THE WEDDING OF

_____ *&* _____

on

_____

My Bride Guide

A Wedding Planner for Your Personal Style

MY BRIDE GUIDE

A Wedding Planner for Your Personal Style

• JUDITH ANN GRAHAM •

BARRICADE BOOKS

Fort Lee, New Jersey

Published by Barricade Books Inc.
185 Bridge Plaza North
Suite 308-A
Fort Lee, NJ 07024
www.barricadebooks.com

Distributed in Canada by University of Toronto Press Distribution

Cover photo by Jeffrey Rothstein

Library of Congress Cataloging-in-Publication Data

Graham, Judith Ann
  My Bride Guide / Judith Ann Graham.
     p. cm.
  ISBN: 1-56980-217-3 (alk. paper)
  1. Wedding etiquette. I. Title.

BJ2051 .G68 2002
395.2'2--dc

200143038

First Printing

Manufactured in the United States of America.

*D*EDICATION:

For

MY MOTHER
EMMA LEE KEITHLEY

Who imprinted me with her strong character
Embraced life's adventures
Resonated an attitude of "I'll try anything once"
And harbors an endless capacity of care and compassion
Her marriage of 53 years
Inspires me to live my life
In the love and light she radiates

For

MY FATHER
ROBERT D. KEITHLEY

Who dazzled me with his brilliance
Instilled the value of being well rounded
Exemplified "I can do anything I set my mind to do"
And carved his life from love and pride
Of all the fathers in the world
I am honored he chose me to be his daughter

To the Bride and Groom:

Throughout this book numerous worksheets are included that will help you create *your* perfect wedding. Given the myriad choices regarding the size and style of your wedding, you may find you need more worksheet space than is provided. Please feel free to photocopy any worksheets you find in this book to better accommodate your needs.

CONTENTS

Contents

CONTENTS

Contents

*I*NTRODUCTION

How wonderful! You—a bride. You float. You glow. You radiate. You beam. You laugh. You cry. You love. You pray. You dream. You wonder. You plan. You begin. You begin a new chapter of life when you marry and your wedding day is the first page. How you create your wedding speaks volumes about you. What's your style? Is it fairy tale or salt of the earth? Is it city chic or home on the range? Is it seaside or mountain peak? Do you picture a full moon or an orange sunset? Can you imagine a pure white snowball wedding or do you smell the colors of each flower in a garden?

No matter what you imagine, you will want help creating the wedding of your dreams. *My Bride Guide* is designed to help you plan with perfection, precision and pride. From your engagement announcement to your reception finale you will be guided by who, what, when, why, where, and how of organizing a great wedding. You will discover ways to announce your engagement with style, assemble a guest list, write heartfelt thank-you notes and utilize the Internet for services, products, and websites. You will learn how to select the perfect officiant and you will discover how to personalize your ceremony.

This book is designed to be your bridal buddy throughout your planning stages. Each chapter is designed to give you ideas and structure, and allow you ample workspace to write estimates, confirm lists and copy contracts. From your first shopping day to your final farewell, you and *My Bride Guide* will become inseparable. All your information will be neatly and conveniently placed at your fingertips. You will save yourself time (a precious commodity for a bride) because you can ask questions and write the answers on your worksheets simultaneously. When you finalize decisions you can copy contract information for easy access and quick reference. All your agreements will be in one place.

Being a bride in the 21st century is demanding and requires a great deal of finesse. As weddings become more involved and relationships more complex, today's bride needs to be an expert hostess and diplomat. Beautiful and confident exuding "grace under pressure" describes a modern bride. Your wedding day is a dream come true. *My Bride Guide* helps you be the bride of your dreams.

WHAT TO LOOK FOR IN THIS CHAPTER:

- Share engagement news first with family and friends closest to you.

- Share the news in person with close family and friends.

- Announce your engagement in your local newspaper and/or develop your own wedding website.

- What to do if you break your engagement.

- 12-month wedding agenda.

Congratulations! You're Engaged

1

> Here's to you both—
> A beautiful pair,
> On the birthday
> Of your love affair.
>
> —*Toasts* by Paul Dickson

You have just said yes to those four little words, "Will you marry me?" You and your fiancé are on Cloud Nine and bursting to tell your friends and family. When you do, you're swept into a whirlwind that compares to nothing you have ever experienced. But where do you begin?

Announcing an engagement is the time-honored custom. Traditionally, it is the time to prepare for the wedding, make your first decisions as a couple, and plan for the future. It's an important time to consider how to share the news of this milestone in your lives with family, friends and community. There is a good deal of joy in organizing your wedding but it also requires painstaking thought, careful planning, and extraordinary attention to detail, beginning with this announcement.

Engagement announcements take on their own personality. Spreading the word to your friends can be as simple as a phone call, but you will still want to follow some basic guidelines. Today people enjoy a casual atmosphere, both professionally and socially. Formal dinners, high teas, and courtly protocol are rare. However, celebrating a wedding can trigger an emotional need to embrace tradition.

Weddings are still solemn events that afford pageantry beyond that of a typical social occasion. The way you make your engagement known will set the tone for the announcements you will make as a couple throughout your lives. Here are some simple suggestions for doing it with grace.

Who to Tell First

Share the good news with your parents and his. A personal visit from you and your fiancé will not only be appreciated, it will make everyone feel good. If it's not possible to tell parents in person then a phone call from both of you is the next best thing. Avoid an e-mail announcement; it's inappropriate.

Next you'll want to share your news with grandparents and siblings. Again, do it in person with close relatives on both sides of the family. Families hear your news first, then friends, then the rest of the world.

If children are involved, announce your engagement to them right away, and include them in your plans. Encourage a dialogue for them to express themselves and allow time for them to adjust to your decision. It is difficult to predict how children will react. Some may be thrilled at the notion of a new mother or father but all will deal with some emotional issues. Time resolves many of them, but the initial announcement can come as a surprise and create special challenges.

Telling the Whole World

You've likely seen the announcements section of any newspaper. It's a good way for couples to formally spread their news. The lifestyle editor of your local newspaper is the person to contact about your engagement announcement. Most have standard forms. Be sure to type or print very clearly. News people are always on deadlines and do not have time to decipher poor handwriting. Get your forms in early, as many papers have lead times as much as six weeks in advance.

Some couples prefer to establish a wedding website when their engagement is announced. You can use this site to direct your friends and family to your registry, showers, parties and agenda..

Ask for the wedding announcement form when you get the engagement form. Wedding notices generally go into more detail about the bride and groom, including schools attended, honors received, occupations, and parents' names, as well as the date and location of the wedding or honeymoon plans. Your paper may charge a small fee for printing the announcements so ask for details.

Don't print your home address, fax, or e-mail addresses unless you want to be barraged with sales calls or unwanted visitors. Follow the instructions precisely regarding forms, photos and deadlines so you will not be disappointed with misprints or, worse yet, nothing printed. Take advantage of websites, e-mails and fax numbers to get the most accurate information about submitting your announcement. Check the wedding section of your paper for an idea of how best to present your photos and information.

A Word to the Wise

Some couples may be intimately involved for years prior to their wedding announcement and a few eyebrows may be raised at their plans for a traditional ceremony. If you happen to be the recipient of comments from thoughtless and opinionated individuals, remember that you have a right to choose the kind of wedding you want.

Your parents will probably be the first to throw you and your fiancé an engagement party. The guest list will require some planning and your help will be appreciated. Engagement parties can take place shortly after your announcement or several months later, depending on the length of the engagement. Many couples choose long engagements, up to a year and a half. This allows plenty of time for many different parties, but the engagement party always comes first.

It doesn't matter if your engagement party is a brunch, tea, lunch, cocktail party, or full formal dinner. That is the decision of your host. What matters is that you invite the close friends and relatives you will ask to your wedding. This is a great time for people to become acquainted. Getting to know each other early on will add to the quality of the day.

ETIQUETTE IN BROKEN ENGAGEMENTS

Occasionally a couple can get caught up in the excitement of getting engaged, then wake up one day to realize they don't want to be married. Should you decide that marriage is not what you want, break the engagement with dignity. Honor your decision even though it will be painful. If your instincts tell you that your marriage is dubious it is better to act on that knowledge now than go through with a costly wedding hoping your doubts will subside.

You will need to notify your clergy official first, then the caterer, florists, musicians, photographers and anyone else you have booked. You can do this by phone. If you have purchased wedding insurance you may recoup some of your deposits. The longer you wait the more it will cost you to get out of your contracts.

Proper etiquette in this situation calls for you to return the ring to him, unless you're wearing your family heirloom. If you have sent wedding invitations, and time permits, send note cards to guests informing them of your decision using this form:

> Mr. and Mrs. Harold Huxley announce
> that the marriage of their daughter, Jane,
> to Mr. Paul Jones will not take place.

If time does not permit, then the personal touch of a note or phone call is best for close family. The use of e-mails or faxes is also acceptable but only as a last resort.

Inform the newspaper that printed your announcement by publishing a retraction along these lines:

> The engagement of Ms. Karen Walker
> and Mr. Tom Fisher has been broken
> by mutual consent

Returning your ring and all engagement and wedding gifts to the givers will demonstrate good taste in an awkward situation, and clear the slate for future developments in your life. No further explanations are necessary.

More than one new bride has related the story of her father's advice in the moments before walking down the aisle, that it is not too late to change her mind. While this is often wishful thinking on the fathers' part, it goes to show you that it is never too late to go back. Cold feet are not the same as wanting out. You'll know the difference. Now, let's proceed with planning the event of your life.

12-MONTH WEDDING CALENDAR

Twelve Months Before the Wedding

- Buy a wedding planner
- Discuss budget and style of wedding with all financially involved parties
- Decide on a date (consider the advice of an astrologer for favorable dates – contact professional astrologer, Shelley Ackerman at *www.karmicrelief.com*
- Book the ceremony and reception sites
- Book the professional services of florist, caterer, photographer, videographer, musicians, wedding consultant
- Choose and ask your attendants (bridesmaids and groomsmen)

Nine Months Before

- Select your officiant
- Register for gifts at stores and online
- Build your wedding website
- Order your wedding dress and all accessories
- Start your guest list (ask both sides of families to compile lists)
- Discuss honeymoon plans and locations

Six to Eight Weeks Before

- Address invitations and mail
- Buy wedding gifts for bride, groom and attendants
- Have formal portrait taken
- Submit announcement to newspapers, update website
- Check requirements for marriage license
- Pick up wedding rings
- Write thank-you notes for gifts
- Make reservations for rehearsal and rehearsal dinner
- Have second fitting for dress; finalize all attire, flowers, accessories for bridal party, mothers, fathers, etc.
- Finalize baker for wedding cake and groom's cake

Up to One Month Before

- Final fittings for bride and attendants
- Inquire about marriage license
- Confirm honeymoon arrangements
- Host Bridesmaids luncheon
- Have bachelor party and bachelorette party
- Confirm contracts with all services for ceremony and reception

Six Months Before	Three Months Before
• Meet with all your wedding professionals to discuss details • Order wedding invitations and stationery and favors • Reserve wedding day transportation • Order bridesmaids' dresses • Make reservations for the honeymoon	• Finalize and complete guest list • Decide attire for groom and groomsmen • Order wedding rings • Call local health department for blood test requirements • Organize accommodations for out-of-town guests • Shop for honeymoon clothes (if necessary) • Book trial hair and makeup sessions • Solidify delivery dates for all dresses and accessories • Buy bridal trousseau, finalize headpiece, have first fitting
Two Weeks Before	**One Week Before**
• Bride and groom get marriage license (in person) • Make salon appointment for facial and hair touch up and trim • Pick up wedding dress and all other attendant's dresses and accessories • Address wedding announcements to be mailed on wedding day • Confirm final guest count with caterer • Make list of must-have photos for photographer and videographer • List musical selections for ceremony and reception - submit to music director(s) • Create wedding programs and print	• Confirm seating arrangements and final head count • Start packing for honeymoon • Finalize details with wedding professionals including wedding consultant • Confirm dates, times and locations with bridal party • Prepare officiant's fee and give to best man • Write checks for remaining balances owed • Have rehearsal and dinner • Keep up with thank-you notes • Be well rested, drink plenty of water and put "relax" on your to-do list

WHAT TO LOOK FOR IN THIS CHAPTER:

- Your role as the honored guest.

- The Engagement Party.

- Bridal Showers and Luncheon.

- Theme Parties.

- Bachelor and Bachelorette parties.

- Personalized Stationery.

- Attendants gift giving.

- Guest list forms for all parties.

2
Prenuptial Parties

> "Make sure whoever is invited to your engagement party is invited to your wedding."
>
> —Carley Roney
> www.theknot.com

THE ENGAGEMENT PARTY

Traditionally the bride's parents are responsible for the first official engagement party. Tradition aside, you can accept an invitation from anyone willing to host. Your job is to provide an up-to-date guest list consisting of close family and friends as soon as possible. Include names, addresses and phone numbers. The function of the engagement party is to facilitate future relationships, since many of its attendees will become family after you marry. As guests of honor, make introductions whenever possible.

WHAT'S YOUR ROLE?

Engagement parties are generally relaxed, semi-casual events. Because they are supposed to give everyone a chance to meet, formal dinners are not common and you need not spend a fortune. Look for creative invitations at Office Depot, Staples or Kinko's or try bridal stationary software packages. The setting is casual—a home, a backyard, a beach house, a barn, or a park. The host can decide what time of day and style of party is best. It could be a brunch, luncheon, cocktail party, or barbecue.

> Be on time.
> Record names and gifts as they are opened.

It is important that you and your fiancé are on time and gracious. You will probably receive a number of engagement gifts, so have a display table available and be sure to record names and gifts as you open them. You do not have to open gifts at the party. But when you do open them, it's a good time to record gifts and thank-you notes in a log that you will keep up throughout your wedding proceedings. The worksheets at the end of this chapter will help you to do this.

Depending on when your party is given, you may receive items from your registry. If you have not registered and you receive gifts you can't use, write a thank-you note and (privately) exchange the item using the gift receipt slip packed within the box. See chapter 5, *Your Wedding Style and Gift Registry* for more information on registering.

THANK-YOU NOTES

If you have personalized note cards use them to thank your guests for your gifts. If you don't, now is the time to order appropriate stationery, as you will have many uses for it during the months before and after your wedding. You need not spend a fortune. Many catalogs and online websites offer handsome note cards at a reasonable cost.

If you want to treat yourself, there are chic stationers like *Smythson of Bond Street* (**www.Smythson.com**), which is located in London and New York. Renowned for creations like Princess Grace's wedding diary, their personalized stationery may be an enormous splurge, but could make a lovely gift for a new bride. That's the high end; there are many levels in between to suit your budget.

You can purchase cards inscribed with "thank you" (the least expensive) or you can order cards with your maiden name or initials. See Chapter 9, *Stationery with Style* for more information.

There's no party like a wedding party, so get ready for a string of them in your honor. Bridal showers, bachelor parties and bachelorette parties are the standard, but your friends may surprise you with their creativity. Theme parties are a favorite and so are "couples showers," which brings us to that time honored custom, the bridal shower.

THE BRIDAL SHOWER

Historically a bridal shower was given to a bride whose father did not approve of her fiancé and as such refused him her dowry. In lieu of the dowry, the bride would acquire her *trousseau* (French for "bundle"), the possessions the bride brings into her new household, through gifts "showered" on her by her female friends.

Traditionally friends, never the family, hosted a shower for the bride and groom. Today, anyone can host a shower. You may find yourself attending showers thrown by your business associates, members of your social circle, school chums or close friends and relatives. Be sensitive to the fact that invitations to the same people for all of the parties will incur extra expense to them. Let them know you'd like them to attend but not buy multiple gifts.

Ask one of the guests to record the giver with a small description of the item on your record of gifts, so you can follow up with appropriate thank-you notes. A favorite bridal

Order personalized note cards.

Get ready for parties galore in your honor.

Bachelor and bachelorette parties are the perfect time to give gifts to the wedding party.

shower tradition is to save the ribbons from the gifts and tie them into a massive bouquet at the end of the party for the bride to use during the rehearsal, or as a momento.

THEME SHOWERS

Shower gifts are usually less expensive than wedding gifts and tend to be more practical. The party is typically a casual, fun event that occurs any time of day. Breakfasts, luncheons, teas or dessert parties are perfectly acceptable. Usually, printed invitations are sent by mail, but phone, fax or e-mail invitations are also common. If it is a theme shower, the invitation should announce the theme and place of registry. Try to register at least six months prior to your wedding as a service to you and your guests. The following gifts are practical but still fun to receive.

> Take advantage of online registries whenever possible. You'll do a favor for both you and your guests.

PERSONAL / LINGERIE

When a couple begins their new life together, they crave small luxuries to make their everyday lives special. Your wish list can contain anything from aromatherapy products to zebra print slippers. One bride was an avid collector of rare perfume bottles and at one of her showers received exactly that—perfume bottles. If pretty lingerie, bath salts and pampering are your thing, drop a hint to your hostess.

LINENS AND THINGS

Sheets, pillows, comforters, duvets, and throws are excellent shower gifts. Register early so your friends know your color scheme. Bath accessories such as his/her towels, tumblers, a waste basket or soap dispenser dress up a bath, but practical items like a bath scale, clock radio or jewelry box are also appreciated, and often overlooked. A combined party, such as a "linens and lace" shower are popular.

KITCHEN

Newlyweds need a host of items for the kitchen. These items come in handy and is not too expensive. If you really want a set of chef's knives now is the time to register for them.

Be forewarned, people shy away from certain kinds of gifts. Most wedding guests have an aversion to purchasing knives for a wedding so if you really have your heart set on something, emphasize what's important to you when your guests inquire. One engaged couple registered for a chainsaw as a wedding gift. They didn't receive it.

On the gentler side, if elaborate cookware is at the top of your list, some of your guests may pool their money. A coffeemaker, juicer, pepper mill or utensils also make wonderful gifts at reasonable prices, as do placemats, napkins and kitchen towels.

BARWARE

Aside from traditional stemware, which ranges from highball to martini glasses, there is a slew of bar products to enhance a couple's home. Consider monogrammed linen cocktail napkins or glass swizzle sticks. Clever bottle stoppers are also nice shower gifts. Ice buckets, wine coolers, water pitchers or sundry bar utensils are always useful.

Unisex Shower

The bride and groom attend this party together. A Jack & Jill shower can consist of a couple's party in your honor, or just a casual get together that includes all of your favorite friends. The benefits are that the bride and groom can celebrate with their male and female friends, who are left out by traditional showers. Today's couples are out in the world as individuals more so than in the past, and have close male and female friends with whom they would prefer to celebrate over a room full of less familiar people who happen to be of the same sex.

Also, gifts can be chosen more flexibly because the shower honors the bride and groom. Favorite CDs, computer accessories, software, cell phones, stereo equipment, or television components can be given, celebrating the activities you enjoy doing together. Cookout gear, skiing equipment, camping equipment, golf/tennis passes or season tickets are also excellent choices.

Despite new trends in prenuptial parties, some old favorites still remain. For example…

The Bachelor Party

> ### The Bachelor's Toast
> In sixteenth century France all ladies of the court were toasted by gentlemen, thus the bachelor party ends when the groom proposes a toast to the bride. The glasses are then thrown over the shoulder assuring that they will never be used again, in a tradition that honors the bride as the bachelor's only love.

Traditionally, bachelor parties occurred the night before the wedding. These days, they are scheduled several weeks prior to the ceremony, replaced, mercifully, by the rehearsal dinner, as the main event for the eve of the big day.

It is not uncommon for the groom to be invited to a bachelor weekend at a favorite hunt club, golf outing, casino or fishing trip. The idea is for him to celebrate his final single days with his favorite pals.

Gifts

The Bachelor party is a good time for the groom to give his attendants appreciation gifts. They are generally the same, although variation in style or color is appropriate as well. Gifts should be moderately priced and have personal meaning. Monogrammed key chains, leather key holders, pen sets, and business card cases set the right tone.

The Bachelorette Party

The groom isn't the only one to enjoy a "final" good time. The bride and her attendants are just as happy to be feted. An old-fashioned slumber party at a weekend retreat is a great way to relax, and bond with your bridesmaids before taking the leap. A current trend is a trip to a day spa that offers a package of beauty services with lunch included.

After all, feeling beautiful in the days leading up to your wedding is part of the fun.

A trip to a bar or two follows in the footsteps of the bachelor party, and is a great way for the immediate female family and bridesmaids to relax and enjoy each other in a casual setting. If you're game, some bridesmaids treat the bride to a male striptease show. Be imaginative, plan a few weeks in advance of your wedding and *have fun*.

The Hen Party

Formerly a British tradition, the hen party has recently appeared in the United States. It's similar to the bachelorette party but requires that the bride be a good sport, as it encourages harmless attention. The evening consists of a pub-crawl, with the bride-to-be adorned in a costume made by her party, which can range from lingerie worn outside the clothes to a T-shirt decorated with lollipops. Be creative, and make sure the attendees are good sports.

Gifts

The bachelorette party is an ideal time to give your bridesmaids their gifts for being in your wedding. Like the groom's gifts, they should be moderately priced and somewhat personal. Many brides and grooms like to give keepsakes. Some suggestions are pearl earrings, complementary evening bags for bridesmaid dresses, a special necklace, or a handmade cross-stitch picture. Consider cosmetic touch up kits from **www.bridalbeauti.com.**

The Bride's Cake

Traditionally a thimble cake is served at the bachelorette party. This is a pink cake with a symbolic thimble or ring baked into it. The one who gets the prized piece of cake is the next bride-to-be. If you do not have a bachelorette party but like the cake, you can incorporate this custom into your shower.

The Bridal Luncheon

The bridal luncheon provides an opportunity to thank your party and the mothers of the bride and groom. It's a nice final get together for women only. Emotions will be running high in anticipation of the day, so a bouquet for the mothers and a nice luncheon will be pleasant for all. You can toast your party and make any last minute thank-yous to all for their help and moral support through your months of planning.

Other inexpensive yet meaningful gifts are pretty stationery or candles. It's semi-casual but slightly dressy, to celebrate a special lunch together at the end of a long road of planning. Keep it simple and enjoyable, as it takes place during the last week or two, and is meant to be a relaxing and fun way to pat each other on the back for a job well done.

PRENUPTIAL PARTIES IN YOUR HONOR

ENGAGEMENT PARTY GUEST LIST/CHECK LIST

Following are spaces to fill in information about invitees and attendees of your engagement party. Should more guests be invited than spaces supplied you can easily photocopy these pages to satisfy your needs.

Name: _____
Address: _____
Phone: _____ Fax: _____ E-mail: _____
RSVP: Yes_____ No _____
Gift:: _____
Date thank-you sent: _____

    ❧   ❧   ❧

Name: _____
Address: _____
Phone: _____ Fax: _____ E-mail: _____
RSVP: Yes_____ No _____
Gift:: _____
Date thank-you sent: _____

    ❧   ❧   ❧

Name: _____
Address: _____
Phone: _____ Fax: _____ E-mail: _____
RSVP: Yes_____ No _____
Gift:: _____
Date thank-you sent: _____

    ❧   ❧   ❧

Name: _____
Address: _____
Phone: _____ Fax: _____ E-mail: _____
RSVP: Yes_____ No _____
Gift:: _____
Date thank-you sent: _____

    ❧   ❧   ❧

Name: _____
Address: _____
Phone: _____ Fax: _____ E-mail: _____
RSVP: Yes_____ No _____
Gift:: _____
Date thank-you sent: _____

Name: _____

Address: _____

Phone: _____ Fax: _____ E-mail: _____

RSVP: Yes_____ No _____

Gift:: _____

Date thank-you sent: _____

⁂   ⁂   ⁂

Name: _____

Address: _____

Phone: _____ Fax: _____ E-mail: _____

RSVP: Yes_____ No _____

Gift:: _____

Date thank-you sent: _____

⁂   ⁂   ⁂

Name: _____

Address: _____

Phone: _____ Fax: _____ E-mail: _____

RSVP: Yes_____ No _____

Gift:: _____

Date thank-you sent: _____

⁂   ⁂   ⁂

Name: _____

Address: _____

Phone: _____ Fax: _____ E-mail: _____

RSVP: Yes_____ No _____

Gift:: _____

Date thank-you sent: _____

⁂   ⁂   ⁂

Name: _____

Address: _____

Phone: _____ Fax: _____ E-mail: _____

RSVP: Yes_____ No _____

Gift:: _____

Date thank-you sent: _____

⁂   ⁂   ⁂

Name: _____

Address: _____

Phone: _____ Fax: _____ E-mail: _____

RSVP: Yes_____ No _____

Gift:: _____

Date thank-you sent: _____

Name: _____

Address: _____

Phone: _____ Fax: _____ E-mail: _____

RSVP: Yes_____ No _____

Gift:: _____

Date thank-you sent: _____

       🌸   🌸   🌸

Name: _____

Address: _____

Phone: _____ Fax: _____ E-mail: _____

RSVP: Yes_____ No _____

Gift:: _____

Date thank-you sent: _____

       🌸   🌸   🌸

Name: _____

Address: _____

Phone: _____ Fax: _____ E-mail: _____

RSVP: Yes_____ No _____

Gift:: _____

Date thank-you sent: _____

       🌸   🌸   🌸

Name: _____

Address: _____

Phone: _____ Fax: _____ E-mail: _____

RSVP: Yes_____ No _____

Gift:: _____

Date thank-you sent: _____

       🌸   🌸   🌸

Name: _____

Address: _____

Phone: _____ Fax: _____ E-mail: _____

RSVP: Yes_____ No _____

Gift:: _____

Date thank-you sent: _____

       🌸   🌸   🌸

Name: _____

Address: _____

Phone: _____ Fax: _____ E-mail: _____

RSVP: Yes_____ No _____

Gift:: _____

Date thank-you sent: _____

Name: _____

Address: _____

Phone: _____ Fax: _____ E-mail: _____

RSVP: Yes_____ No _____

Gift:: _____

Date thank-you sent: _____

❧ ❧ ❧

Name: _____

Address: _____

Phone: _____ Fax: _____ E-mail: _____

RSVP: Yes_____ No _____

Gift:: _____

Date thank-you sent: _____

❧ ❧ ❧

Name: _____

Address: _____

Phone: _____ Fax: _____ E-mail: _____

RSVP: Yes_____ No _____

Gift:: _____

Date thank-you sent: _____

❧ ❧ ❧

Name: _____

Address: _____

Phone: _____ Fax: _____ E-mail: _____

RSVP: Yes_____ No _____

Gift:: _____

Date thank-you sent: _____

❧ ❧ ❧

Name: _____

Address: _____

Phone: _____ Fax: _____ E-mail: _____

RSVP: Yes_____ No _____

Gift:: _____

Date thank-you sent: _____

❧ ❧ ❧

Name: _____

Address: _____

Phone: _____ Fax: _____ E-mail: _____

RSVP: Yes_____ No _____

Gift:: _____

Date thank-you sent: _____

Prenuptial Parties

ENGAGEMENT PARTY GUEST LIST

ENGAGEMENT PARTY GUEST LIST

Name: _____

Address: _____

Phone: _____ Fax: _____ E-mail: _____

RSVP: Yes_____ No _____

Gift:: _____

Date thank-you sent: _____

             ೞ   ೞ   ೞ

Name: _____

Address: _____

Phone: _____ Fax: _____ E-mail: _____

RSVP: Yes_____ No _____

Gift:: _____

Date thank-you sent: _____

             ೞ   ೞ   ೞ

Name: _____

Address: _____

Phone: _____ Fax: _____ E-mail: _____

RSVP: Yes_____ No _____

Gift:: _____

Date thank-you sent: _____

             ೞ   ೞ   ೞ

Name: _____

Address: _____

Phone: _____ Fax: _____ E-mail: _____

RSVP: Yes_____ No _____

Gift:: _____

Date thank-you sent: _____

             ೞ   ೞ   ೞ

Name: _____

Address: _____

Phone: _____ Fax: _____ E-mail: _____

RSVP: Yes_____ No _____

Gift:: _____

Date thank-you sent: _____

TOTAL GUESTS ATTENDING _____

BRIDAL SHOWER PARTIES
(Photocopy as needed for additional guests and parties)

Shower Type (theme): _____

Date: _____ **Time:** _____

Location: _____

Address: _____

Hosted by: _____

       ૐ   ૐ   ૐ

  Guest Name: _____

Address: _____

Gift received: _____

Thank-you note date: _____

       ૐ   ૐ   ૐ

  Guest Name: _____

Address: _____

Gift received: _____

Thank-you note date: _____

       ૐ   ૐ   ૐ

  Guest Name: _____

Address: _____

Gift received: _____

Thank-you note date: _____

       ૐ   ૐ   ૐ

  Guest Name: _____

Address: _____

Gift received: _____

Thank-you note date: _____

       ૐ   ૐ   ૐ

  Guest Name: _____

Address: _____

Gift received: _____

Thank-you note date: _____

       ૐ   ૐ   ૐ

  Guest Name: _____

Address: _____

Gift received: _____

Thank-you note date: _____

Prenuptial Parties

BRIDAL SHOWER GUESTLIST

Guest Name: _____

Address: _____

Gift received: _____

Thank-you note date: _____

❧ ❧ ❧

Guest Name: _____

Address: _____

Gift received: _____

Thank-you note date: _____

❧ ❧ ❧

Guest Name: _____

Address: _____

Gift received: _____

Thank-you note date: _____

❧ ❧ ❧

Guest Name: _____

Address: _____

Gift received: _____

Thank-you note date: _____

❧ ❧ ❧

Guest Name: _____

Address: _____

Gift received: _____

Thank-you note date: _____

❧ ❧ ❧

Guest Name: _____

Address: _____

Gift received: _____

Thank-you note date: _____

❧ ❧ ❧

Guest Name: _____

Address: _____

Gift received: _____

Thank-you note date: _____

Guest Name: _____

Address: _____

Gift received: _____

Thank-you note date: _____

🔔 🔔 🔔

Guest Name: _____

Address: _____

Gift received: _____

Thank-you note date: _____

🔔 🔔 🔔

Guest Name: _____

Address: _____

Gift received: _____

Thank-you note date: _____

🔔 🔔 🔔

Guest Name: _____

Address: _____

Gift received: _____

Thank-you note date: _____

🔔 🔔 🔔

Guest Name: _____

Address: _____

Gift received: _____

Thank-you note date: _____

🔔 🔔 🔔

Guest Name: _____

Address: _____

Gift received: _____

Thank-you note date: _____

🔔 🔔 🔔

Guest Name: _____

Address: _____

Gift received: _____

Thank-you note date: _____

Prenuptial Parties

BRIDAL SHOWER GUESTLIST

Bachelorette Party Worksheet

This is a handy checklist for your attendants who are planning your bachelorette party.

Date: _____   Time: _____

Location: _____

Address: _____

Phone: _____ Fax: _____ E-mail: _____

Contact: _____

Hosted by: _____

Phone: _____ Fax: _____ E-mail: _____

Date invitations sent: _____

Guest List

Name: _____

Address: _____

Phone: _____ Fax _____ E-mail _____

Accept: _____ Regret: _____ Attendant Gift Given: Yes _____ No _____

🐌 🐌 🐌

Name: _____

Address: _____

Phone: _____ Fax _____ E-mail _____

Accept: _____ Regret: _____ Attendant Gift Given: Yes _____ No _____

🐌 🐌 🐌

Name: _____

Address: _____

Phone: _____ Fax _____ E-mail _____

Accept: _____ Regret: _____ Attendant Gift Given: Yes _____ No _____

🐌 🐌 🐌

Name: _____

Address: _____

Phone: _____ Fax _____ E-mail _____

Accept: _____ Regret: _____ Attendant Gift Given: Yes _____ No _____

🐌 🐌 🐌

Name: _____

Address: _____

Phone: _____ Fax _____ E-mail _____

Accept: _____ Regret: _____ Attendant Gift Given: Yes _____ No _____

Name: _____
Address: _____
Phone: _____ Fax _____ E-mail _____
Accept: _____ Regret: _____ Attendant Gift Given: Yes ____ No ____

ðŸ‚ ðŸ‚ ðŸ‚

Name: _____
Address: _____
Phone: _____ Fax _____ E-mail _____
Accept: _____ Regret: _____ Attendant Gift Given: Yes ____ No ____

ðŸ‚ ðŸ‚ ðŸ‚

Name: _____
Address: _____
Phone: _____ Fax _____ E-mail _____
Accept: _____ Regret: _____ Attendant Gift Given: Yes ____ No ____

ðŸ‚ ðŸ‚ ðŸ‚

Name: _____
Address: _____
Phone: _____ Fax _____ E-mail _____
Accept: _____ Regret: _____ Attendant Gift Given: Yes ____ No ____

ðŸ‚ ðŸ‚ ðŸ‚

Name: _____
Address: _____
Phone: _____ Fax _____ E-mail _____
Accept: _____ Regret: _____ Attendant Gift Given: Yes ____ No ____

ðŸ‚ ðŸ‚ ðŸ‚

Name: _____
Address: _____
Phone: _____ Fax _____ E-mail _____
Accept: _____ Regret: _____ Attendant Gift Given: Yes ____ No ____

ðŸ‚ ðŸ‚ ðŸ‚

Name: _____
Address: _____
Phone: _____ Fax _____ E-mail _____
Accept: _____ Regret: _____ Attendant Gift Given: Yes ____ No ____

Prenuptial Parties

BACHELORETTE PARTY GUESTLIST

JACK & JILL COUPLE'S PARTY WORKSHEET

Party Theme: _____

Date: _____ Time: _____

Location: _____

Hosted by: _____

GUESTS

Name: _____

Address: _____

Gift received: _____

Date Thank-You Sent: _____

è& è& è&

Name: _____

Address: _____

Gift received: _____

Date Thank-You Sent: _____

 è& è& è&

Name: _____

Address: _____

Gift received: _____

Date Thank-You Sent: _____

 è& è& è&

Name: _____

Address: _____

Gift received: _____

Date Thank-You Sent: _____

è& è& è&

Name: _____

Address: _____

Gift received: _____

Date Thank-You Sent: _____

 è& è& è&

Name: _____

Address: _____

Gift received: _____

Date Thank-You Sent: _____

 è& è& è&

Name: _____

Address: _____

Gift received: _____

Date Thank-You Sent: _____

🔔 🔔 🔔

Name: _____

Address: _____

Gift received: _____

Date Thank-You Sent: _____

🔔 🔔 🔔

Name: _____

Address: _____

Gift received: _____

Date Thank-You Sent: _____

🔔 🔔 🔔

Name: _____

Address: _____

Gift received: _____

Date Thank-You Sent: _____

🔔 🔔 🔔

Name: _____

Address: _____

Gift received: _____

Date Thank-You Sent: _____

🔔 🔔 🔔

Name: _____

Address: _____

Gift received: _____

Date Thank-You Sent: _____

🔔 🔔 🔔

Name: _____

Address: _____

Gift received: _____

Date Thank-You Sent: _____

🔔 🔔 🔔

Name: _____

Address: _____

Gift received: _____

Date Thank-You Sent: _____

Prenuptial Parties

JACK AND JILL PARTY GUESTLIST

BACHELOR PARTY WORKSHEET

Date: _____ Time: _____

Location: _____

Hosted by: _____

Address: _____

Phone: _____ Fax: _____ E-mail:_____

GUESTS ATTENDING

Name _____

Address _____

Phone _____ Fax _____ E-mail _____

Accept _____ Regret _____ Usher's Gift Given: Yes _____ No _____

❧ ❧ ❧

Name _____

Address _____

Phone _____ Fax _____ E-mail _____

Accept _____ Regret _____ Usher's Gift Given: Yes _____ No _____

❧ ❧ ❧

Name _____

Address _____

Phone _____ Fax _____ E-mail _____

Accept _____ Regret _____ Usher's Gift Given: Yes _____ No _____

❧ ❧ ❧

Name _____

Address _____

Phone _____ Fax _____ E-mail _____

Accept _____ Regret _____ Usher's Gift Given: Yes _____ No _____

❧ ❧ ❧

Name _____

Address _____

Phone _____ Fax _____ E-mail _____

Accept _____ Regret _____ Usher's Gift Given: Yes _____ No _____

❧ ❧ ❧

Name _____

Address _____

Phone _____ Fax _____ E-mail _____

Accept _____ Regret _____ Usher's Gift Given: Yes _____ No _____

Name _____

Address _____

Phone _____ Fax _____ E-mail _____

Accept _____ Regret _____ Usher's Gift Given: Yes _____ No _____

ᴥ ᴥ ᴥ

Name _____

Address _____

Phone _____ Fax _____ E-mail _____

Accept _____ Regret _____ Usher's Gift Given: Yes _____ No _____

ᴥ ᴥ ᴥ

Name _____

Address _____

Phone _____ Fax _____ E-mail _____

Accept _____ Regret _____ Usher's Gift Given: Yes _____ No _____

ᴥ ᴥ ᴥ

Name _____

Address _____

Phone _____ Fax _____ E-mail _____

Accept _____ Regret _____ Usher's Gift Given: Yes _____ No _____

ᴥ ᴥ ᴥ

Name _____

Address _____

Phone _____ Fax _____ E-mail _____

Accept _____ Regret _____ Usher's Gift Given: Yes _____ No _____

ᴥ ᴥ ᴥ

Name _____

Address _____

Phone _____ Fax _____ E-mail _____

Accept _____ Regret _____ Usher's Gift Given: Yes _____ No _____

ᴥ ᴥ ᴥ

Name _____

Address _____

Phone _____ Fax _____ E-mail _____

Accept _____ Regret _____ Usher's Gift Given: Yes _____ No _____

WHAT TO LOOK FOR IN THIS CHAPTER:

- The 3Ps – Paying, Prioritizing, Planning.

- Tips to help limit your wedding costs.

- Questions to ask your officiant.

- Book your ceremony and reception sites.

- Begin to get ideas about other services you will be needing (i.e. florist, baker, etc.).

- Fill in your budget worksheet and priority wish list.

$\mathscr{E}$STABLISHING YOUR PRIORITIES

3

> "Set a budget and stick to it. Money does not equal elegance. Next, prioritize what is important to you, but first lock in the location for the ceremony and reception."
>
> —Gerard J. Monaghan, President
> The Association of Bridal Consultants
> www.bridalassn.com

The role of bride-to-be is an exhilarating, overwhelming and demanding one to play. Everyone will rejoice with you and want to offer well-intentioned advice so it is essential that you sit down with your fiancé to define your wedding. When the opinions of others threaten to overwhelm you, you'll be grounded by your vision of how it should turn out. If you dream of a lavish candlelight ceremony in a medieval castle, your priorities will differ from the bride who cherishes the idea of a barefoot wedding on the beach.

Some couples prefer an intimate setting with a few loved ones, while others won't be happy until their entire hometown is on the guest list. Put yours and your groom's wishes first. You will have to make compromises as you plan your wedding anyway, so if you establish what is important to you and your fiancé firmly, it will ward off a lot of extraneous "help." Use your head, an average wedding cost in the US is $20,000.

THE THREE PS: PAYING, PRIORITIZING, PLANNING

The number one issue in planning a wedding is determining your budget—hardly a romantic topic, but crucial to a successful wedding day. Traditionally the parents of the bride pay for the wedding, however, modern couples frequently receive financial help from other sources. Basically you must decide who is going to pay for it and how.

Once you have decided who pays, you will need a plan. Will it be the wedding of the century or dinner for six? Start with a rough guest list, an approximate crowd number will tell you what kind of money you're looking at, or vice versa.

Establishing Your Priorities

Decide who pays for what.

I know of one couple whose entire wedding was paid for by the guests. The bridegroom was an auto mechanic, known throughout his community. He and his bride announced their engagement two weeks before the ceremony and told their friends by phone. As word spread, the groom's customers began offering their services.

The couple ended up marrying in a church, followed by a formal dinner reception for two hundred guests. The music, flowers, photography, wedding cake, food and beverages were "gifts" from attendees, who were thrilled to participate! So much for drawn-out engagements and expensive weddings....

Incidentally, the entire affair took place in New York City, where costs are sky-high and spaces are booked at least a year in advance! So anything is possible.

ALL IN THE FAMILY

As news of your engagement spreads, some friends or relatives will offer their professional services. This is a great way to have your cake and eat it too! It helps to have a hairdresser, printer or baker in the family. Be sure you know exactly what you are getting, and

Which family / friends can you call in to offer their professional services?

that the quality of service meets your standards. If you suspect the product or service is not what you want it's better to politely refuse the offer by saying you already have it covered.

SPONSORSHIP

A more creative approach to financing an expensive wedding is to solicit sponsors. If you or your fiancé is an aggressive marketer with natural selling skills this could be an option. With today's fierce wedding competition, some vendors feel they can better reach clients through non-traditional advertising methods. Ask local vendors for gratis or reduced fee services for your special day in exchange for displaying their name at your reception. If you are proud of the work, you'll be eager to let everyone know who's responsible for it. Young couples are usually among a wide circle of peers that marry within a couple of years of each other, so a sponsor's donation in exchange for name exposure is a valuable collaboration for both sides. Be prepared to have the names of your sponsors printed on your wedding program, display brochures, and wedding favors.

Sponsorship is not for everyone. Don't be surprised if some businesses give you a cool response. Incidentally, most etiquette experts agree this method is inappropriate.

THE PENNYWISE BRIDE

Consider unique ways to limit costs.

Nowadays, the cost of getting married can equal a down payment on a home. It is foolish and unwise to go into debt for a wedding day. If you and your fiancé have limited finances, consider the following suggestions:

- Rent a bridal dress. The selection is good if you start early and allow time for fittings. You can rent a couture gown for a fraction of the cost of owning it.
- Choose an off-season to get married. Ask your local hotels when they are at low occupancy.

- Get married in late morning and have a lunch reception. Generally, lunch menus are less expensive and guests tend to consume less liquor.
- Serve wine or beer. Avoid the cost of a full bar setup.
- Limit your guest list. If you're the primary financial source, give your family and his a finite number of guests.
- Hire a disc jockey instead of a band.
- Serve a sit-down lunch or dinner. It is less expensive than a buffet.
- Have a champagne reception with dessert and wedding cake in late afternoon.
- Plan the rehearsal dinner at home or have a backyard barbecue.
- Make favors for guests and gifts for attendants by hand.
- Shop online for great values on wedding supplies from accoutrements to honeymoon vacations.

THE OFFICIANT

The next priority after working out your financial plan is to begin your bookings. Start by making an appointment with your officiant. He or she will want to meet with you and your fiancé, and will be able to tell you what dates are available for your ceremony. This and the availability of a reception site are often the guiding forces behind setting your date.

> Start booking your officiant now.

An officiant is the person who presides over your wedding ceremony. It can be a minister, judge, priest, rabbi, clergy person, justice of the peace, or mayor. He/she will give you specific advice about the wedding ceremony and advise you of your legal responsibilities. If you are marrying in a foreign country you will need to have a civil ceremony in order to be legally married. Remember, marriage requires legal documentation in the form of blood tests and a license. See chapter 15, *Legal Ease*, for more information.

Many couples are of different faiths and look forward to seeing both their religions represented. If you are considering an interfaith wedding, by all means get opinions from both clergy. Choose the site where you will be married and be sure the officiants are in agreement with one another, and available on your wedding day. Let them know whether you are having a double or single ring ceremony.

Discuss how to personalize your ceremony with your fiancé and officiant well in advance of your wedding. Have you written your own vows or are you following a standard ceremony? If you and your fiancé have a favorite poem discuss it with your officiant and decide who will recite it.

The best ceremonies blend elements of the bride and groom's personality. A special song or traditional custom to honor your/his heritage can be incorporated, or if your marriage is bi-cultural, you may want to request two officiants. Your wedding is an opportunity to express not only your love for one another, but the uniqueness of each, as you blend your lives. Your cultures are important to you, and you can pay tribute to them both if you do it right.

QUESTIONS TO ASK YOUR OFFICIANT:

Ask your officiant about dos and don'ts.

- Which days are prohibited to perform certain religious ceremonies?
- Is secular (non sacred music) permitted?
- What is the policy regarding live vs. recorded music? Are you required to use the designated music director or organist?
- What are the rules for photographers and videographers?
- What floral arrangements are advisable and where? After the ceremony should the flowers remain or can they be transported to the reception? Sometimes a floral donation is appreciated at the site.
- What is the policy for candlelight ceremonies?
- Are aisle decorations permitted? Can you use an aisle runner and if so who supplies it—the site or the florist?
- Will you be seated during the ceremony? Will you be kneeling? What about kneeling cushions?
- Will extra chairs be needed? Who supplies them?
- What are the regulations regarding canopies or a Chuppah?

OTHER PRACTICAL CONSIDERATIONS...

- Ask about the use of Bibles, wineglasses, or personal items during the ceremony.
- Request a review of the ceremonial text.
- Ask what the officiant(s) will wear. Find out if they will attend the reception.
- If the reception is being held at the site, inquire about adequate cooking facilities, restroom facilities, parking arrangements, and dressing room facilities with sufficient lighting, mirrors and security.

See chapter 6, *Choosing the Perfect Officiant*, for more information on your meeting.

THE SITE

For the ceremony, consider the scale and size of the site selected. Consider the number of guests; it should look full but not crowded. Avoid enormous cathedrals if you have a small crowd.

Ceremony and reception sites should complement one another.

Your reception site should reflect your ceremony. A formal wedding is best accompanied by a dinner in a similarly formal setting. Conversely, a beach ceremony can be accompanied by a cookout. They should compliment one another. Attention to these details will create a blueprint for the rest of your planning. See chapter 8, *Your Reception Blueprint*.

Finding an available site will seem like one of your biggest challenges. Remember that once you've settled this issue, all others will fall into place. Availability ranges, depending on the length of your engagement. A popular site can have a waiting list as long as two years during a popular season like spring or autumn, but will be able to offer more reasonable rates and availability if you are willing to compromise with a winter or weekday reception.

Consider your guests' needs. Do they need to stay overnight? Is a weekday reception impossible to attend due to work? Are they traveling? If so, a winter wedding could result in a poor turnout, or worse, getting stuck somewhere.

These considerations are as instrumental in picking your space as its availability. No matter how much you love a reception site, it is a nightmare for you if you can't afford it, can't wait for an opening, or can't accommodate your friends and family.

Your wedding is a chance to see many dreams realized, but this choice requires you to be practical. Do your homework, make a lot of calls, and don't be persuaded by banquet managers that want to talk you into a site that doesn't suit you. You will be working closely with them to plan your day and you have to feel good about them. Remember, your reception is their business.

INVITATIONS

Once you know when and where, you're ready to think about invitations. Many gift shops and stationers offer this service. Ask if you can bring sample books home, and plan an afternoon looking through them. You'll be surprised at the variety of styles. See chapter 9, *Stationery With Style* for details.

> Stationery reflects your style of wedding.

MUSIC

Whether or not you've decided between a DJ or a band, peruse the yellow pages, newspapers and bridal fairs for music sources. If you have recently-married friends, their referral or, better yet, your experience at their reception will put you on the path to choosing and booking music for your reception. Depending on where you plan to marry scheduling music can be as challenging as booking a room, but don't be afraid to interview a couple of companies to be sure you get what you want. See chapter 10, *Music, Music, Music,* for more information on how to choose your music.

> Decide on live vs recorded music.

PHOTOGRAPHY / VIDEOGRAPHY

It all goes by so fast. Be sure you have a record of this remarkable day. If you feel being filmed will prevent your absorbing the moments in real time, then forego the video and go with still photos. If you have family and friends that can't be there, an unobtrusive videographer will bring your party to life over and over again in the future. A good photographer will capture you and your guests in the best light, with artful composition—an irreplaceable rendering of your special day. So whether you choose one or both, be certain to meet with them, check out their wedding experience, and most of all look at samples of their work. A real bonus is finding a photographer that allows you to own your negatives. See chapter 11, *Picture Perfect*, for more information.

> When it's all over you will be left with memories and great photos.

The Florist

Flowers add romance.

The flowers at your ceremony and reception provide a beautiful creative outlet for the bride. If you can book a florist that operates in the same town as your bakery, it will make it easy for you to consult with both. A popular trend is a cake decorated with fresh flowers, and if you go this route they will need to work with one another. A good florist can establish the mood of your wedding from the moment guests enter the church, so look at their books and know their reputation. At the very least, you will need them for your bouquets, boutonnieres, church flowers, cake and reception centerpieces. See chapter 12, *Fabulous Flowers*.

The Cake

Gone are the days of the white sponge wedding cake, bearing plastic figurines. Today's cakes are festooned with ribbons and flowers, shaped any way you choose, separated into spiraling tiers, and flavored any way you want. If you choose traditional white, go for a design that inspires awe. Do you have a favorite birthday cake? Tailor it to your wedding style. The art of cake making enjoys its finest moments in the wedding cake, and can extend to the rehearsal dinner (i.e. groom's cake) and/or bridal shower. See chapter 13, *Wedding Cake Wonders*, for the best way to choose your bakery.

Transportation

Will it be by a limousine or a bicycle built for two?

You should decide well ahead of time how you will be arriving at and departing from your wedding. No doubt you will want to provide transportation for the bridal party and special family members. It's too early to plan who gets driven where, but that doesn't preclude booking a limousine or car service. They will draw up a contract and take a deposit so you know you're set for that day. The balance can be adjusted closer to the wedding, when you confirm your plans. Many places will accept final payment as late as two weeks before the ceremony. At least book them and set your mind at ease.

As the day approaches, make a list of who is to be transported and have it ready for your transportation host. Specify to the driver where the guests are to go for the ceremony and reception (include directions and phone numbers.) Ask your bridal party to congregate at a central location for easy pickup. Make sure you hire a reputable company and solidify all details, as this small aspect of the day can throw it out-of-whack if it's done wrong.

At one wedding the groom hired two buses to transport his large out-of-town family to the ceremony and reception. Transportation to the ceremony went fine, everyone was on time, but the reception was a different story. The second bus lost the first bus and arrived more than two hours late for the reception. The bus driver as it turned out, spoke no English and therefore could not understand either written or spoken directions.

Fortunately, the reception cocktail hour took place on a gorgeous evening outdoors. Needless to say plenty of cocktails were served while waiting for the absent guests to arrive. As for the absentees, they wisely convinced the driver to pull into a roadside hotel where they started their own cocktail hour while waiting for a new driver to rescue them.

Although the reception worked out in this case, it's never wise to let guests drink too much too soon. Remember, they probably haven't eaten in quite some time. Do your best to be present on the heels of cocktail hour to begin the reception. Even your banquet manager will be anxious to get you there, and get your guests seated, to insure a freshly served meal. Keeping your festivities moving along will insure that the day is well paced.

MENTAL HEALTH

If you've begun to make the necessary calls to wedding services, asked friends to participate in the party, and told loved ones of your plans, then no doubt you're beginning to feel some stress. Your biggest priority throughout the process of planning your wedding is to maintain your sanity. A good way to remain calm and composed while keeping your wedding plans under control is to make your own physical and mental needs as important as anything else.

Take a holiday from stress!

Exercise, hobbies, work—all are factors of your normal life. They were priorities before your engagement and they will be there when you begin married life, so use them to keep you grounded and release your stress when the "happiest day of your life" threatens to overwhelm you. A successful wedding is one that expresses your joy. If you allow yourself to unravel over the months leading up to it, you may find yourself in tears instead. Remember: it's an important day, but it's only one day in your lifetime.

Establishing Your Priorities

ESTABLISHING YOUR PRIORITIES WORKSHEET

Fill in the blanks, make copies, and have one handy at all times.

Wedding Budget Estimate
How much: $_____

Who is footing the Bill?

Bride _____ Groom _____ Bride's parents _____ Groom's parents _____ Other _____

How much is each contributing?

Bride _____ Groom _____ Bride's parents _____

Groom's parents _____ Other _____

Style of Wedding desired (Circle one):

Very formal   Formal   Semiformal   Informal

Ceremony Site

House of worship   Hotel/hall   Outdoor site   Historic site   Home

Choice of Officiant

Minister   Priest   Rabbi   Judge

Mayor   Interfaith Minister   JP

Reception Site

Hotel/banquet facility   historic site   home   outdoors

Guest List

Fewer than 50   50-100   100 –150   150 – 200   over 200

Wedding Priority Wishlist
Rank in order of importance from most important to least important.
Most important- 5, Important- 4, Average Importance- 3, Not very important- 2, Least important- 1.

Traditional Ceremony

5   4   3   2   1

Non-traditional Ceremony

5   4   3   2   1

Inclusion of Ethnic customs and traditions

5   4   3   2   1

Ceremony site

5   4   3   2   1

Reception site

    5   4   3   2   1

Destination wedding

    5   4   3   2   1

Wedding weekend

    5   4   3   2   1

Large guest list

    5   4   3   2   1

Small guest list

    5   4   3   2   1

Food, cake and beverages

    5   4   3   2   1

Flowers

    5   4   3   2   1

Music

    5   4   3   2   1

Photography/videography

    5   4   3   2   1

Gown

    5   4   3   2   1

Large bridal party

    5   4   3   2   1

Small bridal party

    5   4   3   2   1

Transportation

    5   4   3   2   1

WHAT TO LOOK FOR IN THIS CHAPTER:

- Choose your bridal party carefully (including child attendants).

- 12 attendants in total is sufficient.

- Advise attendants of their duties.

- Go over best man duties with groom.

- Review ushers' duties.

- Have one usher for every 50 guests.

- Find a way to include special people who are not part of the bridal party.

- Plan separate activities for child attendants.

THE BRIDAL PARTY

Most likely the first thing you thought about when you became engaged was who you wanted to stand up with you. Before you decide, remember that your wedding party plays a pivotal role in your ceremony and adds to the mood at your reception. They will also be the first faces your family and friends see at the church, so consider your representatives.

Your attendants should be the honor guards of your wedding. They are there to help you and the groom get through the day smoothly and pick up the slack before and after it. Consider this very seriously. When you take an honest look at them, do you see a responsible generous friend that you have always been able to count on? If you're not sure, then perhaps they're better left to the guest list.

Once you make your choices, include them in your plans from the start. The best way to help your attendants help you is to be well organized. Knowing what you need from them is the next best thing to doing everything yourself. Once the wedding day arrives you will be pulled in many directions and you must be able to count on your attendants to keep an eye on your personal belongings and your appearance.

One bride took responsibility for everything and arrived at the church with an all-purpose bag containing everything from makeup for touch-ups to headache medicine. A well-meaning guest spirited the bag away as she entered the church and promptly forgot about it. By the middle of the reception, her makeup was smudged, her hair wild, and the touch-up bag nowhere to be found. A responsible attendant would have called her attention to her appearance but unfortunately the busy bride never saw herself until the reception photos revealed a very wilted bride. What's more, the morning after was rough without aspirin! With today's hotel receptions, the bride's day does not end at the church—most likely you will be waking up in a honeymoon room at your reception site, and amenities will be of utmost importance. Your attendants are your right arms for all such detail.

Because it is such an important job, your party usually consists of close friends or family members. Select your attendants keeping in mind the time and financial expenses. Aside from special duties there are considerable costs such as tuxedo rental, bridesmaids' dresses, shoes, etc. A real friend will be honored to share your day whether she is *in* your party or *at* your party.

By the same token, don't be offended if someone refuses to be part of your wedding. They may have a valid excuse, such as cost, time, prior commitments or personal problems that are no reflection on you. Respect their willingness to be honest with you rather than letting you down later.

The number of attendants is your choice though 12 is quite enough by today's standards. Bear in mind that a large party will multiply your responsibilities, and can make the ceremony look busy. You don't want to get lost in the crowd. Following is a suggested list of traditional wedding party attendants and their duties:

FEMALE HONOR ATTENDANT—

MAID OF HONOR / MATRON OF HONOR

This person is anyone with whom you share a special relationship. Usually she is your best friend or a sister, but that doesn't rule out a favorite aunt or grown daughter. It is best not to have your mother as an honor attendant since she already has the distinction of being Mother of the Bride. Your honor attendant has duties beyond those of the rest of your bridal party.

HONOR ATTENDANT DUTIES

- Hosts or co-hosts a bridal shower for you.
- Helps with prenuptial planning such as trousseau shopping, gown selection, addressing and stuffing invitations, etc.
- Wedding day duties include keeping you calm, helping you get ready, making sure you eat before the wedding and handling last minute details.
- Ceremony duties include adjusting your train and veil, holding your bouquet at the appropriate times and carrying the groom's ring. She is your legal witness and must sign the marriage certificate.
- Reception duties involve offering a toast to the newlyweds (if you ask), taking care of your gown by bustling the train, detaching your veil if you wish, touching up your hair or makeup and helping you change from your gown into your going-away apparel. She will also make sure wedding gifts are transported to a designated location.
- Responsible for purchasing dress and accessories selected by the bride.

BRIDESMAIDS

You may opt solely for a maid/matron of honor. Most brides, however, choose an average of four attendants—one honor attendant and three bridesmaids. Twelve attendants are considered the maximum.

BRIDESMAIDS' DUTIES

- Host or co-host a bridal shower and the bachelorette party.
- Help perform wedding tasks such as preparation of wedding favors and rice packets, arrange transportation for out-of-town guests, address invitations, etc.
- Responsible for purchasing individual bridesmaid dress, shoes and other accessories the bride chooses.

> **Traditional Folklore**
> The tradition of the bridesmaid comes from ancient Greece. Originally bridesmaids were married women who would protect and shower the bride with good luck and blessings for her future, and fertility.

DRESSES

Ultimately, the decision is yours. Your bridesmaids are obligated to at least wear the color and style chosen by you. It's your decision whether to shop with them, which will help you understand what styles suit whom, or simply tell them what to order. If you make the choice by yourself, consider their coloring, body types, and ages. An old-fashion tradition is to dress the maid of honor in a different style or color. This can be done quite tastefully and sets her apart. See chapter 14 *Bridal Gowns and Wedding Apparel*.

A great way to keep the costs down is to shop off the rack in the formals section of a department store. The garment quality exceeds that of a typical bridal shop dress, and can be worn again. Current trends are separates and slightly different styles on each woman. Each woman is complemented by the style that's most appropriate for her and the cookie cutter bridesmaid look is eliminated.

See chapter 12, *Fabulous Flowers*, for information on bridesmaids' bouquets.

JUNIOR BRIDESMAIDS

Age 8 to 14, these maids are included in the bridal party not to exceed 12 attendants. They usually wear a less sophisticated version of the bridesmaids' dresses. Junior bridesmaids do not need a male escort for the ceremony.

BEST MAN

For this honor, the groom selects his best friend, a brother, his father, grown son, or relative. The groom may also choose a "best woman" to be part of the bridal party. She could have the full honor or simply usher.

BEST MAN DUTIES

- Host or co-host the bachelor party or bachelor weekend.

- Lend moral support to the groom.
- Keep ushers and groom on schedule.
- Hold the bride's wedding ring and sign the marriage license as a witness.
- Propose the first toast to the newlyweds and relay any telegrams, faxes, e-mails of congratulations.
- Arrange the return of rented formal attire.
- If necessary, arrange transportation to the airport for the couple.
- Organize the "just married" car decorations.
- Disperse "tip" envelopes for the groom.

MALE HONOR ATTENDANT

Some women have male best friends. If your best friend is a man, ask him to be in your bridal party as the bride's best man. Give him special responsibilities that will not make him uncomfortable and be sure to advise your professional staff (caterer, photographer, musicians, etc.) of his status. Invite him to sit at the head table and ask him to prepare a toast. He can wear the same clothing as the ushers.

Don't be surprised if your fiancé asks a special female friend to be in the bridal party. Such was the case at a wedding, where the female was a close friend of the groom's family. The groom asked her to wear a ladies tuxedo and assume the role of usher. She was thrilled, and the groom felt he'd included her in a distinct and honorable way. A female usher could also choose a dress that coordinates with the ushers' tuxes, but sets her apart from the bridesmaids.

USHERS' DUTIES

- Help host or co-host the bachelor party.
- Seat guests as they arrive for the ceremony.
- Distribute programs and rice or petal sachets to guests.
- Make sure all guests have transportation and directions to the reception. Should it rain, ushers provide umbrella escorts to cars.
- Help decorate the couple's wedding car.
- The head usher provides special assistance to disabled guests or seats divorced parents. He also examines the ceremony site before leaving, for any forgotten items.

Plan to have one usher for every fifty guests. Guests of the groom are seated on the right side of the room and guests of the bride on the left side in a Christian wedding (the opposite in a Jewish wedding). If you have junior ushers, have them pass out wedding programs. Most churches employ wedding coordinators to advise ushers about the best way to seat guests and to advise latecomers whether it's a safe moment to slip in quietly.

A coordinator will either advise them to spread guests over the space available, or recommend that the ushers "pack 'em and stack 'em." A small crowd grouped together may make the church seem half empty, but if all are good friends, it's refreshing to take in the sea of faces during your processional.

On that note, there is a way to savor such an opportunity. If your officiant is flexible, you may want to incorporate a brief moment into the ceremony where you and your fiancé may look back and take in your crowd. One minister asks couples to stop and look back at the guests, as a way of savoring the rare moment standing before their friends to be joined in marriage. It also gives everyone a chance to see you, since the rest of the ceremony is spent with your backs turned.

JUVENILE ATTENDANTS

Children in a wedding can be either adorable or intolerable. An older child age five to eight is probably fine. Younger children, three to four, are less predictable. Consider the age and maturity of the children you are inviting to be in your wedding. Surrounded by festivities and excitement, children are usually removed from their normal schedule and don't get enough rest. Try to avoid late night rehearsal dinners and request a "nap time" the day of your wedding. During the reception provide a sitter, a separate room, kids menu, games and videos. These provisions encourage the kids to enjoy their own party, and you can enjoy yours.

FLOWER GIRL
This little tot carries a basket of flower petals, which are tossed on the bridal path. The petals signify fertility and blessings for the bride.

RING BEARER
This child is usually a boy. He carries a satin pillow with symbolic rings sewn on. Often the ring bearer and flower girl walk together. The best man and maid/matron of honor hold the authentic wedding rings, to be exchanged during the ceremony.

ADDITIONAL ATTENDANTS
Weddings are a celebration of love and goodwill. If you sense you have disappointed someone by not inviting him/her to be in your wedding party, find a way to include them. A little creativity and generosity of spirit goes a long way toward making your wedding day special for all of your guests.

The happiest weddings encourage loved ones to participate. One couple, previously married, asked their children and grandchildren to sing a favorite song during the ceremony. A chorus of twelve adults and children delighted everyone by singing a touching song that added special meaning and included both families.

If you have people you really want to include, here are some additional jobs or honors:

READER
Ask them to read a poem or scripture that is special to you. Choose carefully; don't just

pick something to get them up there. The purpose of a reading is to express your feelings about this union, and should be in keeping with the character of your ceremony.

PRESENTATION ROSE

Hand a rose or present a flower from your bouquet to a special person as you make your way down the aisle.

TRAIN BEARERS

Extremely formal weddings may feature two small children to follow the bride, carrying her cathedral length train as she makes her way down the aisle. These "pages" maintain the direction of the train, insuring a graceful walk down the aisle.

CANDLE ATTENDANTS

This can be someone special to you or it can be an altar boy or girl. They light designated candles prior to the mother of the bride being seated. After the service they extinguish the candles.

The Bridal Party

BRIDAL PARTY WORKSHEET

MAID OF HONOR

Name: _____

Address: _____

Phone: _____ Fax: _____ E-mail: _____

Arrival Date: _____

Duties: _____

_____

_____

MATRON OF HONOR

Name: _____

Address: _____

Phone: _____ Fax: _____ E-mail: _____

Arrival Date: _____

Duties: _____

_____

_____

BRIDESMAIDS

Name: _____

Address: _____

Phone: _____ Fax: _____ E-mail: _____

Arrival Date: _____

Duties: _____

_____

_____

❧ ❧ ❧

Name: _____

Address: _____

Phone: _____ Fax: _____ E-mail: _____

Arrival Date: _____

Duties: _____

_____

_____

Name: _____
Address: _____
Phone: _____ Fax: _____ E-mail: _____
Arrival Date: _____
Duties: _____
_____
_____
_____

≈ ≈ ≈

Name: _____
Address: _____
Phone: _____ Fax: _____ E-mail: _____
Arrival Date: _____
Duties: _____
_____
_____
_____

≈ ≈ ≈

Name: _____
Address: _____
Phone: _____ Fax: _____ E-mail: _____
Arrival Date: _____
Duties: _____
_____
_____
_____

≈ ≈ ≈

Name: _____
Address: _____
Phone: _____ Fax: _____ E-mail: _____
Arrival Date: _____
Duties: _____
_____
_____
_____

≈ ≈ ≈

Name: _____
Address: _____
Phone: _____ Fax: _____ E-mail: _____
Arrival Date: _____
Duties: _____
_____
_____
_____

BRIDAL PARTY WORKSHEET

The Bridal Party

Name: _____

Address: _____

Phone: _____ Fax: _____ E-mail: _____

Arrival Date: _____

Duties: _____

_____

_____

❧ ❧ ❧

Name: _____

Address: _____

Phone: _____ Fax: _____ E-mail: _____

Arrival Date: _____

Duties: _____

_____

_____

❧ ❧ ❧

Name: _____

Address: _____

Phone: _____ Fax: _____ E-mail: _____

Arrival Date: _____

Duties: _____

_____

_____

❧ ❧ ❧

Name: _____

Address: _____

Phone: _____ Fax: _____ E-mail: _____

Arrival Date: _____

Duties: _____

_____

_____

BRIDAL PARTY WORKSHEET

The Bridal Party

GROOM'S WORKSHEET

BEST MAN

Name: _____

Address: _____

Phone: _____ Fax: _____ E-mail: _____

Arrival Date: _____

Duties: _____

_____

HEAD USHER

Name: _____

Address: _____

Phone: _____ Fax: _____ E-mail: _____

Arrival Date: _____

Duties: _____

_____

_____

GROOMSMEN / USHERS

Name: _____

Address: _____

Phone: _____ Fax: _____ E-mail: _____

Arrival Date: _____

Duties: _____

_____

_____

☙ ☙ ☙

Name: _____

Address: _____

Phone: _____ Fax: _____ E-mail: _____

Arrival Date: _____

Duties: _____

_____

_____

THE BRIDAL PARTY

Name: _____
Address: _____
Phone: _____ Fax: _____ E-mail: _____
Arrival Date: _____
Duties: _____
_____
_____

ॐ   ॐ   ॐ

Name: _____
Address: _____
Phone: _____ Fax: _____ E-mail: _____
Arrival Date: _____
Duties: _____
_____
_____

ॐ   ॐ   ॐ

Name: _____
Address: _____
Phone: _____ Fax: _____ E-mail: _____
Arrival Date: _____
Duties: _____
_____
_____

ॐ   ॐ   ॐ

Name: _____
Address: _____
Phone: _____ Fax: _____ E-mail: _____
Arrival Date: _____
Duties: _____
_____
_____

ॐ   ॐ   ॐ

Name: _____
Address: _____
Phone: _____ Fax: _____ E-mail: _____
Arrival Date: _____
Duties: _____
_____
_____

The Bridal Party

Name: _____
Address: _____
Phone: _____ Fax: _____ E-mail: _____
Arrival Date: _____
Duties: _____
_____
_____

☙ ☙ ☙

Name: _____
Address: _____
Phone: _____ Fax: _____ E-mail: _____
Arrival Date: _____
Duties: _____
_____
_____

☙ ☙ ☙

Name: _____
Address: _____
Phone: _____ Fax: _____ E-mail: _____
Arrival Date: _____
Duties: _____
_____
_____

☙ ☙ ☙

Name: _____
Address: _____
Phone: _____ Fax: _____ E-mail: _____
Arrival Date: _____
Duties: _____
_____
_____

GROOM'S WORKSHEET

The Bridal Party

OTHER PARTICIPANTS

RING BEARER

Name: _____ Age: _____
Duties: _____
Functions to attend: _____
Adult in charge: _____
Address: _____
Phone: _____ Fax: _____ E-mail:_____
Arrival Date: _____

FLOWER GIRL

Name: _____ Age: _____
Duties: _____
Functions to attend: _____
Adult in charge: _____
Address: _____
Phone: _____ Fax: _____ E-mail:_____
Arrival Date: _____

READER

Name: _____
Address: _____
Phone: _____ Fax: _____ E-mail:_____
Arrival Date: _____
Reading: _____

PERFORMER

Name: _____
Address: _____
Phone: _____ Fax: _____ E-mail:_____
Arrival Date: _____
Performing: _____

CANDLE BEARER

Name: _____
Address: _____
Phone: _____ Fax: _____ E-mail:_____
Arrival Date: _____

TRAIN BEARER

Name: _____
Address: _____
Phone: _____ Fax: _____ E-mail:_____
Arrival Date: _____

WHAT TO LOOK FOR IN THIS CHAPTER:

- The four styles of weddings.

- How to register for gifts.

- Getting the most from your registry.

- White elephant gifts.

- Requesting cash or unusual gifts.

*Y*OUR *W*EDDING *S*TYLE AND GIFT REGISTRY

Wedding styles can follow a variety of themes, but most couples choose a combination of traditional and modern flourishes to give their day a personal touch. This section deals with the traditional types of ceremonies, and offers suggestions for variations on the theme.

There are four established wedding styles. It is important to note that the one you choose reflects your personal tastes, budget and customs. Personalizing your wedding is what gives it special meaning.

REGISTERING

This wedding style chapter ends with advice for registering. Just as a wedding's type of ceremony evolves from the personalities of the couple, so does their registry reflect their lifestyle. Are you starting from scratch, or do you share a home already? Are you an older couple or just out of school? Do you prefer cash for a nest egg, or household gifts to start a new life or refresh the old one? Is your ceremony casual and intimate, discouraging expensive gifts, or formal and traditional, precipitating future heirlooms like china or crystal? With these themes in mind, let's begin at the beginning.

Weddings reflect your lifestyle tastes.

FOUR TRADITIONAL WEDDING STYLES

EXTREMELY FORMAL

The ceremony is held at a religious site such as a temple, church, synagogue or cathedral. The reception is held in an equally lavish setting, a private club, hall, elaborate restaurant, hotel, opulent home, or even a cruise ship. The guest list tops 200.

The dinner or buffet consists of several courses preceded by a cocktail hour. Stationery is engraved and includes at least a reception card, a response card, and pre-stamped envelope.

Table settings consist of fine china and silver with elaborate floral displays. A live orchestra performs music. There is one usher for every 50 guests, a large bridal party, including a maid/matron of honor and a best man.

Also included are bridesmaids, groomsmen, and, optionally, flower girl and ring bearer. Formal portraits are taken of the bridal party and families. Professional bridal consultants are usually hired to oversee the entire event.

Cost: Very Expensive.

FORMAL

This style uses elements of the extremely formal but allows more flexibility in application.

A religious site may or may not be used. It is appropriate to hold the wedding and reception in the same building, provided it is an exquisite site. The same rules as stated in extremely formal style apply to stationery and the bridal party.

Food service is still elaborate but table dressing is less formal. Again, one usher to every 50 guests is adequate. (This ratio is standard.) As a general rule, up to 12 attendants; including children, in either style wedding is considered appropriate. Anything bigger is excessive. A bridal consultant is frequently hired.

Cost: Expensive to Very Expensive.

SEMI-FORMAL

This is a more relaxed style but still follows certain etiquette. A ceremony at a religious site generally takes place during the day, with a reception to follow. A religious location is not required.

Engraved invitations are appropriate. A separate reception card is not required—you may indicate the reception on the response card with self addressed stamp.

Handwritten invitations are passé. If you do not have enough time before the date to print and mail invitations, a personal phone call is recommended. Semi-formal weddings are usually not as large as formal or extremely formal weddings. A minimum of two attendants is necessary; a maid/matron of honor and best man, but up to six attendants is okay. Generally the bride chooses a less formal gown.

Menu, flowers and music are at the bride's discretion. Often a DJ is hired, as opposed to live music. Wedding décor is simplified. You may eliminate any formalities that seem out of place at a semi-formal wedding. Traditional formal photography can be replaced with photojournalism, i.e. more candid shots.

Cost: Moderately Expensive.

INFORMAL

None of the previously mentioned rules apply to an informal wedding, however it is important to respect marital customs to give the occasion the solemnity it deserves, and is tastefully appointed.

Remember, above all, that you are planning a wedding not a birthday party. An outdoor ceremony can be held at a beach, forest, a mountaintop, or any sort of special location. By the same token, it could be held in a home or favorite restaurant. The informal wedding usually takes place during the day among a few good friends and relatives.

Computer generated invitations are acceptable, as are phone calls. The bride can select a simple suit or daytime dress. Wedding décor, music and formal photography are optional.

Cost: Moderate.

(For more on about your wedding style, see chapter 14, *Bridal Gowns and Wedding Apparel*)

REGISTERING FOR GIFTS

For most brides, the bridal gift registry is one of the most detailed activities when planning your wedding. Fortunately, today's bride has many registering options compared with years ago. Begin by asking your fiancé to join you on a shopping spree to choose items for your home together. Most men are not patient shoppers, so you may want to do a preliminary tour to determine what type of items you need and want in your environment. This way your shopping is focused by the time he joins you.

> Register in stores and online. Don't hesitate to register for non-traditional gifts.

Using store bridal registries, online registries, and a consultant is advisable, especially if you have a large guest list. Some couples feel awkward about gift registries but bear in mind that guests expect to give you a gift and appreciate a registry as exemplary of your tastes. You will also eliminate the problem of duplications.

Most couples register at more than one store for variety. You may choose traditional department stores or jewelers for fine china and crystal, and at your favorite hardware/appliance store for audio and video equipment or garden furniture. Fine china and crystal selections are best made with the help of a consultant. A major store with a bridal department can help you with the number of settings and accessories you might otherwise overlook.

One couple I worked with felt registering for gifts was overwhelming and time consuming so they asked the mother of the bride to register for them. Unfortunately, they not only received piles of unwanted gifts, but found exchanging them an even bigger hassle. They also faced an embarrassing moment when a guest visiting their home asked where they placed the "chosen" stemware pattern she'd enjoyed buying them.

POINTS TO REMEMBER ABOUT GIFT REGISTRY:

- Be sure you understand the store's return/exchange policy and the time frame allowed.
- Register for more gifts than you think you need. Many brides under-register and live to regret it. Guests also complain that few items are left on the registry.
- Register for expensive and inexpensive items. Some people pool together for a big gift, and small items make great shower gifts.
- Make use of the store's online registry and be sure your guests from out-of-town know about it as well.
- Tell your mother and friends where you have registered so they can include the information with your shower invitations. It eliminates unnecessary calls.
- Ask for weekly updates of your gift registry or track your progress online. You can always have your updates faxed to you.
- Many couples prefer practical gifts in lieu of traditional gifts. Consider registering at stores such as *The Home Depot, Walmart* or *Taget*.
- Gift etiquette is important to implement.

HOW TO RETURN AND EXCHANGE GIFTS:

Duplications will occur, and you will receive at least one questionable gift. What to do? Send a thank-you note to the sender immediately and then quietly exchange the gift for something useful. The best time to do this is after the wedding when you know which items will complete your gift registry.

Damaged gifts must be reported to the store immediately. The sender does not have to be informed unless the gift was insured, in which case they will be responsible for collecting the insurance to replace the gift.

Almost every couple has the close relative who chooses not to select from the registry and gives a seemingly ridiculous gift. Keep it and send a gracious thank-you note. When the person visits, display the gift then put it away after they leave.

You never know. In one incident, a bride received a ratty looking rug from her mother-in-law. She rolled it up and threw it in the basement. Twenty years later she re-discovered it, and had it appraised. Today the antique Persian rug is one of her prized possessions. With a new appreciation of its true value, she prominently displays it in her dining room.

CASH GIFTS AND UNUSUAL GIFTS

Many guests believe it is unimaginative and in poor taste to give cash to the bride and groom. Depending on your circumstances you may consider the following points before formally requesting money. If you go that route, be sure to indicate what you will use it for in your thank-you note to the sender. Whatever your decision, be certain to register for gifts as well as make your case for cash gifts.

> If you request cash be sure your thank-you specifies how it will be used.

POINTS TO CONSIDER WHEN ASKING FOR MONEY:

- Cash should be put toward a life-enhancing gift.
- Cash should ideally be put toward a large ticket item such as a house, car or completing an education.
- Cash should be requested in the spirit of acquiring essential life enhancing items, not just the latest computer or stereo equipment. Ask yourself, is all this money going toward an item we need or simply want?
- If intended for a nest egg, take your official marriage license to the bank to open a joint account. Guests usually make a point to write out a check to "Mr. And Mrs." Without an account, the money will not be accessible without both endorsements and a source to back up the checks.

Some couples determine that they would like unusual gifts. In such instances you may receive one of these gifts at a bridal shower if you hint strongly enough, but don't be surprised if such an item isn't purchased from your bridal registry.

If your financial circumstances deem large gifts unnecessary, you may opt to inform your guests. Your guests will act accordingly. You may still receive nontraditional gifts such as antique artifacts, museum quality art, collector glass works, or one-of-a-kind handmade keepsakes.

YOUR WEDDING STYLE AND GIFT REGISTRY WORKSHEET

Use this chart as a final checklist for your gift registry.

Formal China   Pattern _____   Mfr. _____

Formal Flatware   Pattern _____   Mfr. _____

Formal Stemware   Pattern _____   Mfr. _____

Casual Dinnerware   Pattern _____   Mfr. _____

Casual Flatware   Pattern _____   Mfr. _____

Casual Stemware   Pattern _____   Mfr. _____

Additional Serving Pieces (i.e. trays, bowls, coffee service, etc.)

_____

_____

_____

_____

_____

_____

_____

_____

Barware

Pattern _____   Mfr. _____

Bar tools _____

Accessories _____

Kitchen

Cookware Mfr._____

Bakeware Mfr._____

Cutlery Mfr. _____

Appliances (toaster, can opener, etc.) _____

Utensils _____

Plastic Ware _____

Wooden Accessories _____

Other _____

Linens

Bed Linens _____

Bath Linens _____

Bath Accessories _____

Table Linens _____

Decorative Objects (lamps, clocks, candlesticks, etc.) _____

_____

_____

_____

_____

Stationery _____

_____

_____

Luggage _____

_____

_____

Furniture _____

_____

_____

Electronics _____

_____

_____

Home Appliances & Equipment _____

_____

_____

ANNIVERSARY GIFT CHART

Year	Traditional	Modern	Year	Traditional	Modern
1	paper	clocks	15	crystal	watches
2	cotton	china	16	sterling	sterling or plate, silver hollowware
3	leather	crystal and glass			
4	linen	electric appliance	17	furniture	furniture
5	wood	silverware	18	porcelain	porcelain
6	iron	wood	19	bronze	bronze
7	wool	desk set	20	china	platinum
8	bronze	linens and lace	25	silver	sterling silver jubilee
9	pottery	leather	30	pearl	diamond
10	tin, aluminum	diamond jewelry	35	coral, jade	jade
11	steel	fashion jewelry, accessories	40	ruby	ruby
12	silk	pearl or colored gem	45	sapphire	sapphire
13	lace	textile and fur	50	gold	golden
14	ivory	gold jewelry	55	emerald	emerald
			60	diamond	diamond

WHAT TO LOOK FOR IN THIS CHAPTER:

- How to find the best officiant for your needs.

- Checklist of pertinent questions to ask your officiant.

- What gets included in a wedding program.

- Worksheets to guide you while working with your officiant.

6
CHOOSING THE PERFECT OFFICIANT

> *Many, many hundreds of hours are put into the preparation of a wedding that quite often becomes a huge production. Marriage, however, is the biggest decision in life and the marriage ceremony is often entered into without much preparation. A wedding is one day—a marriage is for life. The marriage vows still state, "until death do us part."*
>
> —Father Maurice K. O'Mahony
> Pastor, Our Lady of Mount Carmel Parish
> Montecito in Santa Barbara, California

Your wedding ceremony is a proclamation of the bond you share with one another. Whether you are religious or not, your ceremony is an opportunity to weave tradition, love and your own spirit into a meaningful service. Choosing an officiant is the most important aspect of planning your wedding. It takes patience, planning, persistence and commitment from both of you. A wedding ceremony is the most sacred commitment of your life together and marks an event unequal to any other.

You may be one of a few brides that knows who your officiant will be. If so, consider yourself lucky. Many brides and grooms face a challenge in our multi-cultural society finding the right person to perform their ceremony. Today there are many options for finding the right person to sensitively administer your wedding vows.

Look for the right officiant to represent you and the groom.

In one instance a bride married a man whose family spoke very little English. Aiming to please her future in-laws, she found a bilingual minister so the service could be recited in both languages. She and the groom hired the minister outside the church and had the ceremony in a hotel. The minister was Lutheran, the groom Catholic, and the bride Protestant.

Another couple decided to get married in France. She was Catholic and he was Muslim. Both lived in England but wanted to be married in the famous St. Germain des Prés Church in Paris. After some in-depth inquiry, they found a Priest to perform the ceremony even though neither one lived in France, nor were members of the church or religion.

Choosing the
Perfect Officiant

HERE ARE SOME SUGGESTIONS RANGING FROM TRADITIONAL TO ALTERNATIVE.

- **Religious affiliated.** If you are a member of a local house of worship and you both agree to be married by a specific religious figure, speak to that individual. In most cases either you or the groom knows the officiant. It is a simple matter of determining date, time and location. Ask if there are any religious "block out dates" such as Passover in the Jewish faith or fasting periods of Eastern Orthodox religions. Chances are one or both of you are raised in the same faith. This is generally the smoothest religious ceremony between two people who have not been married. If one of you is divorced check with your officiant regarding church-sanctioned annulments or religious divorce decrees. Ask about premarital counseling encouraged by some faiths.

- **Religious unaffiliated**. Perhaps you and the groom want a religious ceremony but you are not affiliated with a house of worship. Decide what is important to the two of you. If you are planning your wedding overseas or in an unfamiliar location, ask

> Determine the degree of religiousness you want from your officiant.
>
> Don't compromise spirituality in your ceremony.

friends, family and local wedding consultants for advice. Find out which houses of worship welcome marriage ceremonies from nonmembers. Sometimes local religious business listings indicate sites that are available and can be rented for a fee. Check out local officiants who perform weddings outside the "church." Chances are you can hire the officiant without being members, and have your ceremony in a neutral place.

- **Dual Religious Ceremony.** There are growing numbers of couples who prefer to have both religious backgrounds represented. In these cases, having officiants from each religion to perform a ceremony is important to them. If you and your fiancé are in this category, start by asking your local clergy if they are willing to marry you in a dual ceremony. These days it is not unusual to find reform rabbis performing ceremonies jointly with Catholic priests. You may be surprised at the flexibility of many clergy.

  Check your sources and ask in your community for advice. Nearly all communities have nondenominational sites where you can get information pertinent to your situation. What once was forbidden in combination marriages is rapidly becoming more commonplace.

- **Interfaith.** Some couples decide to downplay their religious backgrounds and opt instead for an Interfaith service. Anything but anti-religious, qualified ordained Interfaith Ministers tailor each ceremony with divine purpose. The emphasis is on customs, traditions and rituals that promote spirituality rather than religion. As the world becomes more unified, more people consider themselves spiritual, not necessarily religious. An Interfaith service often soothes the religious misgivings of traditional-minded family members while satisfying the spiritual needs of the wedding couple.

As described by the Association of Interfaith Ministers, interfaith means:

1. A dialogue or cooperation between major faiths.
2. Union of two or more spiritual paths in a specific context (i.e. an environment that honors both traditions).
3. Spirituality at the deepest level by means of which all religions have evolved.

You can locate Interfaith Ministers and Clergy through ethical cultural societies, a Unitarian Church, a nondenominational chapel, a university ministry office or via the Internet at the Association of Interfaith Ministers—www.interfaithclergy.org.

According to Rev. Laurie Sue Brockway, an Interfaith Minister, "ceremonies are conducted in the spirit of 'Interfaith.' They are traditional/nontraditional, non-denominational, mystical and symbolic. They contain elements, rites and rituals from one or many traditions, including Judaism/Kabbalah, Christianity, Hinduism, Buddhism, Taoism, Islam/Sufism, Shamanism and Native American Spirituality. Also included are Goddess Spirituality, the Essenes, the Celts and the Ancient Egyptians."

CIVIL CEREMONY

A Justice of the Peace, a Judge, or a Mayor performs a civil ceremony. These ceremonies contain no religious overtones and contain only the legal language to satisfy marriage requirements. If you know a Judge, etc., then it is up to his/her discretion to "dress up" the service. The city or town hall where you want to be married is your first stop to find out when and what time services are conducted. The local license bureau that issues marriage licenses is your best bet to find out who is qualified to perform marriage ceremonies. Even if you elope it is recommended that you interview officiants before you decide who will marry you.

> Legal wedding ceremonies contain no religious overtones.

A SELF-STYLED CEREMONY

Some couples choose to write their own ceremonies. You must still have an officiant to legally marry you, but you can recite your personal feelings and expressions, and include traditions and customs in your ceremony. Acknowledge children if you or your spouse have them from previous marriages. Use poetry, scriptures or appropriate verses to add meaning. Although a handcrafted ceremony is generally less formal and smaller than a formal one, it does not mean your style should be. There is no such thing as a casual wedding.

> There is no such thing as a casual wedding.

FINALIZING DETAILS WITH YOUR OFFICIANT

By now you probably feel comfortable with your officiant. Still, there are some final questions that should be discussed to make your ceremony special and personalized. Review the following for clarity.

- Reserve the site and establish costs. Firm up the date and time of the ceremony. Are there other ceremonies on the same day? Does the officiant have other ceremonies to conduct? Will he/she be attending the rehearsal and reception, alone or accompanied? What are their names?

- Review the format of the ceremony. Discuss processional and who, if anyone, will escort the bride. Will she be given away? Where will the groom, best man and ushers stand?

- Go over prayers and readings. Can you omit or rewrite outdated wording? Who will recite what? Who will be performing and when? Will you be incorporating traditions, or customs into the ceremony? Lighting candles, sharing a cup of wine, etc.?

- Review the bride and groom's vows. When will you stand and face each other? Will you be sitting, kneeling, standing, facing the altar, backs to guests during the ceremony? What variations will you use?

- Will the officiant help mediate differences between divorced parents? What about advice for children from previous marriages? Can he/she help resolve challenges with adoption issues, deadbeat parents, or deaths in the family? As concerns arise during the wedding planning, is the officiant available for counseling?

- Will the officiant deliver a homily or address? If so, how long? How long is the total service? What is the officiant's fee? Are there other fees for additional employees at the site? Is tipping accepted? If so, how much is suggested?

- If for some reason you doubt the credentials of your officiant, call the organization of his/her faith and ask if he/she is a member in good standing. Ask if you can attend a ceremony where he/she is officiating. Find out the fee and agree on a deposit.

WEDDING PROGRAMS

Once you have made the final decisions for your ceremony you may want to write a program for your guests. The purpose is to acknowledge those in your bridal party by name and position, establish the ceremony format, and list readings, music, prayers, etc. by author and performer. The cover page can be elaborate, with a photo or drawing, or simple, with just your names. You can print a favorite prayer on the back page or share your own special message. Ask your officiant for sample wedding programs to get ideas. You can have them printed or you can have them done economically on computer and copied.

Wedding programs outline the events and participants in the ceremony.

In the future, you will enjoy reading through your program and remembering those moments. It's one of the best ceremony keepsakes you will own, especially if you spent the time to make your ceremony meaningful.

CHOOSING THE PERFECT OFFICIANT WORKSHEET

OFFICIANT

Name: _____

Address: _____

Phone: _____ Fax: _____ Email: _____

Fee: _____ Deposit/Date: _____ Final Payment/Date: _____

Best time to call: AM _____ PM _____

CEREMONY RULES & REGULATIONS

Readings permitted: yes _____ no _____

Recommendations: _____

_____

_____

Music permitted: yes _____ no _____

Recommendations: _____

_____

_____

Placement of photographers: _____

_____

_____

Candle Lighting: _____

_____

_____

Sitting/standing/kneeling – where & when: _____

_____

_____

_____

Homily/address: _____ How long: _____

What topics would you like mentioned in the address?: _____

_____

_____

_____

Bride's vows: _____

_____

_____

_____

_____

_____

_____

_____

Groom's vows: _____

_____

_____

_____

_____

_____

_____

_____

Ring exchange: _____

_____

_____

_____

_____

_____

_____

_____

OTHER CONSIDERATIONS

Ceremony Site

Date site reserved: _____ Time: _____ Cost: _____

Parking: _____

_____

Directions: _____

_____

_____

_____

_____

_____

Aisle runners: _____

_____

Canopies: _____

_____

Flower placement: _____

_____

_____

Flowers: Remain _____   Remove _____

Extra chairs: _____

Waiting room for bridal party: _____

_____

Area for receiving line: _____

_____

Other: _____

_____

_____

_____

_____

_____

ASK YOUR OFFICIANT

Perform Rehearsal (in person):   yes _____   no _____

Date: _____   Time _____

Attend Rehearsal Dinner: yes _____   no _____

Attend reception: yes _____   no _____

How many: _____

Names of guests: _____

_____

Officiant's Attire: _____

Available for Counseling: yes _____   no _____

WHAT TO LOOK FOR IN THIS CHAPTER:

- A full rehearsal of the ceremony will set your mind at ease on your wedding day.

- Tips to make your rehearsal go smoothly.

- Little details make a big difference—checklist of what to remember.

- Seating arrangements for Christian and Jewish ceremonies.

- Processional and recessional order for Christian and Jewish ceremonies.

- Receiving line options and order of appearance.

- Handling potential problems.

- Origin of ceremony traditions.

- Write it all down—worksheets to help make your ceremony a lasting memory.

A Ceremony to *R*emember

7

> *Love is the epiphany of God in us.*
> —Thomas Merton

The Ceremony Rehearsal

The ceremony rehearsal is the best time to receive answers to last minute questions, air your concerns and hear others', however, it is important to go in with a plan. If you are too open to suggestions your participants' ideas will confuse you. The rehearsal is meant to give you and your wedding party confidence. A rehearsal lets everyone know what to do and when to do it, that's all.

If possible, plan your rehearsal two to three days in advance of your wedding. After all, it is your final chance to hammer out details and last minute changes. Rehearsals the day before can be stressful, leaving you tired and anxious on your wedding day.

Practice makes perfect.

Again, the key to a successful wedding is throwing one that is enjoyed by all, especially the bride and groom. Make the following considerations your priority to help guarantee a pleasant, organized ceremony.

Who attends?
1. Officiant
2. Parents/guardian(s) and your fiancé's parents/guardian(s)
3. Wedding party: bridesmaids, ushers, honor maid/matron, best man, child attendants

4. Anyone you have asked to participate, such as candle lighters, readers, musicians

5. Your wedding coordinator, if you have one

REHEARSAL PREPARATION TIPS

• Rehearsals should finalize your plans, not initiate a sudden burst of creativity.

• Practice with whoever will walk you down the aisle. In Christian ceremonies the bride's father traditionally escorts her. In Jewish ceremonies, both parents escort the bride, and sometimes, the groom.

• Discuss who will sit where and who will need an escort. This is particularly important if parents are divorced. Don't leave out second time spouses just because they are not blood relatives.

• Take a small bouquet and faux rings to the rehearsal. Make sure you pass the bouquet comfortably to your honor attendant. You may want to wear your wedding shoes to break them in.

• Put a little Vaseline on the interior of your rings so they will slide on easily. Do it with both wedding bands on the rehearsal day so you don't need to think about it the day of your wedding.

• Discuss duties with ushers. Go over seating instructions; designate who will roll out the aisle runner and who will escort your mother. Be sure they know where coat racks, rest rooms and fire exits are located.

  Make sure all ushers have extra printed directions to the reception if necessary.

• Designate where the wedding participants meet prior to the wedding. Appoint the time you want the ushers to arrive to begin seating guests. They are usually expected 45 minutes to an hour prior.

• Give the marriage license to your officiant.

DETAILS MAKE THE DIFFERENCE

Although your officiant will guide you through the ceremony, telling you when to sit, stand, kneel, or cross, it's a good idea to be aware of what you will be doing. Ask if you will be seated during the ceremony or if you will stand. If you decide to light altar candles practice crossing and passing the candles. Ask your readers to practice the approach to the podium. Ask for the microphone to be turned on and volume levels adjusted. If amateur musicians are requested to sing or play an instrument, ask them to perform their selections at the rehearsal using all necessary equipment. In other words, make sure your participants' needs are met as well as your own.

Take time to rehearse the entire ceremony from beginning to end.

What's in a Reading?

Your officiant will help you select particular readings. If you have favorites from Holy Scriptures, traditional poetry or prose, incorporate it into the ceremony. Readings add a special meaning that customizes your ceremony to your ideas of love and marriage.

> Readings are an expression of your love.

Christian Ceremony

Seating Arrangements

Assuming your church has a center aisle, the bride's guests are seated to the left (as you face the altar) and the groom's guests are seated on the right. If the church has a center section with aisles to the left and right the same procedure is observed.

- Reserve pews in the front of the church for family, relatives and special friends— particularly those doing readings. The first several pews are usually reserved with decorative wreaths, flowers, or ribbons. You can consult your florist.

- If you expect a large turnout, print pew cards and enclose them with your invitations. Otherwise, mail pew cards after you have received your replies.

- Your parents and his are always seated on the first row on their respective sides (bride to the left / groom to the right). If your gown has a long train be sure your escort is on your left side so he does not cross in front of you or step on your train trying to get to his seat.

- The second pew is reserved for grandparents and siblings.

- The third pew is for relatives, parents of small child attendants and specific friends.

- Ushers seat the guests from the front to the back.

- Women are always escorted, their male counterparts walk behind. Older women are seated first if a group arrives.

- Late guests seat themselves. If they arrive after the church door is closed, they can slip in after the bride has walked down the aisle.

- Once all the guests have been seated the ushers take their places (at the altar in a Catholic ceremony or at the rear of the church in a Protestant ceremony).

- The last person seated is the mother of the bride. She takes her seat of honor on the first seat of the first pew on the left side. When she is seated it is an indication the procession is at hand. It begins when the mother stands, signaling the guests to stand, and the processional music to start.

TRADITIONAL CHRISTIAN CEREMONY

PROCESSIONAL

Father of the Bride & Bride

Flower Girl & Ringbearer

Maid of Honor

Bridesmaids

Ushers

Best Man & Groom

Officiant

POSITION AT THE ALTAR

Ushers

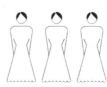

Bridesmaids

Ring Bearer

Flowergirl

Best Man

Father of Bride & Maid of Honor

Groom & Bride

Officiant

RECESSIONAL

Officiant

Groom's Mother & Father

Bride's Mother & Father

Bridesmaids & Ushers

Maid of Honor & Best Man

Flowergirl & Ringbearer

Bride & Groom

TRADITIONAL JEWISH CEREMONY

PROCESSIONAL

Bride's Mother | Bride | Bride's Father

Flowergirl & Ringbearer

Maid of Honor

Bridesmaids

Groom's Mother | Groom | Groom's Father

Best Man

Ushers

Rabbi

POSITION AT THE CHUPPAH

Bridesmaids

Bride's Parents | Groom's Parents

Maid of Honor | Best Man

Bride & Groom

Rabbi

RECESSIONAL

Rabbi

Ushers & Bridesmaids

Ushers | Maid of Honor & Best Man

Flower Girl & Ringbearer

Groom's Mother & Father

Bride's Mother & Father

Groom & Bride

PROCESSIONAL

Order of Appearance

1. The officiant resides at the altar. The groom and best man stand to the right of the altar. Sometimes the officiant leads the groom and best man down the aisle. Ask for the protocol at your church.
2. The ushers walk from the rear of the church according to height and stand next to the best man. If you have an odd number of bridesmaids or ushers have the shortest one walk alone.
3. Bridesmaids are the next to walk. Pair them up if you have more than four.
4. Junior bridesmaids follow the bridesmaids. If you have two or more, pair them.
5. Next comes the maid or matron of honor. The one with the most duties stands the closest to you.
6. Child attendants are last to walk before the bride. If your flower girl sprinkles petals on the runner she can follow the ring bearer.
7. The bride enters with her father or designated escort on her left arm.
8. If you have pages they follow the bride to "carry" the train.

RECESSIONAL

You enter singlely, and exit a couple. Overall, everything works in reverse order and everyone is paired. Here are some guidelines.

1. The bride and groom lead the exit from the altar.
2. Flower girl and ring bearer – paired.
3. Maid/matron of honor and best man – paired.
4. Bridesmaids and ushers—in pairs.
5. The bride's mother and father, followed by the groom's parents. If you prefer, an usher may return to escort the mother of the bride/groom.
6. The officiant is the last to leave.
7. The guests leave from front to back.

JEWISH CEREMONY

SEATING ARRANGEMENTS

The biggest difference between a Jewish ceremony and a Christian ceremony is that the bride and her guests are seated on the right and the groom and his guests on the left. Also, the parents and grandparents stand at the Chuppah. A Jewish ceremony involves more of the immediate family than does a Christian ceremony. The row seating for guests follows the same as a Christian ceremony. Mind you, these are traditional directions.

PROCESSIONAL

1. The rabbi and cantor begin the procession. The cantor is on the rabbi's right.
2. The bride's grandparents followed by the groom's grandparents are next. Men are on the left, women on the right.

3. The ushers are next (in pairs according to height—from short to tall.)

4. Best man.

5. The groom enters escorted by his mother and father—father on groom's left, and mother on the right.

6. Bridesmaids; if you have more than four pair them. If you have an odd number have the shortest proceed alone.

7. The maid or matron of honor is next. The one with the most duties walks last.

8. Ring bearer.

9. Flower girl.

10. Finally, the bride proceeds escorted by her parents. The bride's father is on her right and mother is on her left.

11. Guests remain seated during a Jewish ceremony.

RECESSIONAL

1. Leading the recessional is the bride and groom. Bride on right, groom on left.

2. The bride's parents follow them, mother on right, father on left.

3. Next come the groom's parents, following the same procedure: females on right, males on left.

4. The ring bearer and flower girl are next, paired together.

5. The best man and maid/matron of honor follow the child attendants.

6. The ushers and bridesmaids proceed, paired together.

7. The recessional ends with the cantor and rabbi's exit—cantor on rabbi's left.

THE RECEIVING LINE

A formal receiving line at a large wedding can be overwhelming—for both the wedding party and the guests. First, decide how you want to receive your guests. If you opt for the formal receiving line it is advisable to form a line at the reception site. That way, some folks can mingle and others can sit down, etc. If you choose to have a receiving line at the ceremony site be sure the area is large enough to accommodate everyone.

One way to coordinate a receiving line with rice throwing and an extemporaneous exiting photo, is to receive your guests at the back of the church or site before leaving the building. The guests proceed from your line to wait outside where they receive petals, rice, or seed for throwing as you emerge. This not only gives your photographer a good set up, it also gives your guests an opportunity to photograph you together in the flush of your happy moment.

RECEIVING LINE ORDER

Traditionally, the mother of the bride is at the beginning of the receiving line, followed by the bride's father, then the groom's mother, and the groom's father. You are next, the bride and groom. Next to the groom stands your honor maid/matron, then your atten-

> Beat the receiving line blahs—have guests blow bubbles or you can release a box of butterflies, white doves, etc.

dants. The best man generally does not participate in the receiving line. If you want to condense the receiving line you can ask all the parents to mingle with guests. You can eliminate your attendants as well.

More and more couples are choosing a Chinese custom, which encourages the bride and groom to visit each table briefly at the reception for a quick greeting and thanks to each of the guests for attending. If you don't know some of the guests, then introduce yourself and your husband.

A nice approach was one taken by the bride, who, blessed with perfect weather, chose to have her receiving line outdoors. Once the guests were outside, she opened a box of monarch butterflies and let them flutter away. The effect was unique, romantic and photogenic. It also was a natural icebreaker—everyone was pleasantly surprised, and she was able to greet her guests in a timely fashion, with something to talk about.

REHEARSAL PROBLEM SOLVING

Nearly every couple encounters unforeseen situations at their rehearsal. The most obvious scenarios revolve around some of the wedding party being unable to attend. In these cases have a stand-in, who must then advise the absentees. If you have a wedding coordinator he/she will see that the matter is handled.

> Be gracious and sensitive to feelings.

Use your judgment as to whether child attendants should be included at your rehearsal. If you believe the children will perform better with practice then invite them. If an impromptu performance is best, then forego the rehearsal. By all means make sure children get proper rest. Overly tired, fussy children can put a damper on your wedding day and can frazzle your nerves.

Finally, be sure your extended family is handled sensitively. If your parents are divorced be sure the new spouses or significant others are included. Make sure women are properly escorted and desirably seated. If one of the parents is deceased ask a grandparent or special relative to stand in their place. If you or your fiancé are adopted and have a relationship with your birth mother or father decide how you will handle their participation at your wedding—assuming they accept your invitation.

If you anticipate someone "showing up" who is not an invited guest speak with your wedding coordinator, officiant, or a discreet family member about being prepared to ask them to leave. If it's discussed briefly at rehearsal, it will eliminate melodrama that distracts from the wedding day.

WEDDING CEREMONY TRADITIONS

Reprinted with permission from **www.interfaithweddings.com**/*customs.htm*

Wedding Banns

This is an announcement of an impending wedding in the Catholic Church. This announcement usually takes place for three consecutive Sundays. Its purpose was to inform the public with enough notice of the pending wedding so if anyone objected to the marriage, they could do so.

Wedding Ring

The marriage ring represents a promise for eternal and everlasting love. It is a representation of the promises joining both the bride and groom together. The wedding ring is placed on the fourth finger of the left hand because it was traditionally believed that this finger was a direct connection to the heart—the perfect spot to place a symbol representing eternal love and commitment.

Altar Positioning

This tradition dates back to the time when marriage might take place by capture. By having the bride stand to the groom's left, the groom would have his right hand free for his sword if he needed it for defense.

Arch of Swords Following Ceremony

Walking through the arch of swords following the ceremony was done to ensure the couple's safe passage into their new life together.

Breaking of Glass

A Jewish tradition that represents the destruction of the temple in Jerusalem. Many times couples save the pieces of glass from the ceremony in a symbolic box.

Bridal Gown (White)

There was a time when the bride would wear her favorite dress to the ceremony. In 1840, Queen Victoria wore an elegant all white gown to her wedding. She started a fashion trend which quickly caught on and continues to this very day. White was worn because people believed it represented affluence, virginity and purity.

Bridal Veil

Traditionally the bridal veil was a symbol for modesty, respect and virginity. The veil served as a reminder to all witnessing the ceremony that the physical relationship was entered into only after the vows were exchanged and the marriage became official with the seal of a kiss. The veil was removed after the vows were exchanged and the couple was pronounced "Man and Wife."

Child Attendants

Children were originally included in the ceremony to evoke innocence and impending fertility.

Father Giving the Bride Away

This custom originally had it's roots in arranged marriages where the bride was considered property. Later, this custom persisted as a symbol with two meanings:
- An endorsement by the father to all witnessing the ceremony that the groom is the best choice for his daughter.
- An offering to the groom: "I am presenting to you my daughter."

Flowers and the Tossing of the Bouquet

Flowers were incorporated into the ceremony because they represent fertility, purity, new life, and never ending love. Traditionally, bouquets were a mixture of flowers and herbs. Dill was a very popular choice as an herb because it was believed to promote lust. Following the ceremony, the dill was eaten for that purpose.

Groom Entering Church First/Groom Exchanging First Vow

Both of these customs signify that the groom is the covenant initiator. Because he is the initiator, he is the first to state his vow for marriage. As the initiator of the covenant, the groom is to assume the greatest responsibility in the marriage.

Chuppah

In the Jewish religion, the ceremony takes place as the couple stands under an ornamental canopy. This canopy symbolized nomadic tents of Israel and the new home that the couple would soon share.

Kiss

No ceremony is complete without the kiss. In fact, there was a time when an engagement would be null and void without one. Dating back from early Roman times, the kiss represented a legal bond that sealed all contracts.

Pronounced "Man and Wife"

This is the point of time when the marriage becomes official. It is also at this point that the bride officially changes her name.

Signing of Wedding Papers and the Signing of the Guest Book

The signing of the marriage certificate documents a public record of the marriage. The guest book was a record of all the people who witnessed the wedding. For that reason, the guest book is supposed to be signed following the official wedding ceremony.

Something Old, Something New, Something Borrowed, Something Blue

You may have heard the saying that the bride is to wear "something old, something new, something borrowed, and something blue." And, although you know that most brides perform this ritual, you're probably wondering why they do this and what it means. Each part of this saying holds some form of traditional significance. The old and new items represent the passage from the single status to the married status. The borrowed item represents the participation and approval of the wedding by family, friends, and the community. Something blue is a symbol of purity, love, and fidelity. In England, this saying goes on further to include "...and a lucky sixpence in your shoe" which brides will still do.

Taking of Each Other's Right Hand

The open right hand is a symbol of strength, resource, and purpose. The coming together of both right hands is a symbol that both the bride and the groom can depend on each other and the resources that each brings to the marriage. It also represents the merger of their lives together into one.

Throwing of Rice, Flowers

When thrown as the couple exited the church, the throwing of rice and flowers represented the wish for the couple to have a fruitful and plentiful life together. Originally rice and wheat were thrown over the married couple to represent the hope of fertility.

When rose pedals are thrown before the bride as she walks down the aisle, it is to ward-off evil spirits below the ground and grant fertility.

Unity Candle

The unity candle is a symbol of family unity. Usually a single candle (representing the newly married couple) is lit with two individual candles, each representing the bride's and groom's families.

White Aisle Runner

The white aisle runner symbolized God's holiness and walking on holy ground. It is believed that marriage is not just between two individuals but includes the presence of God who is actively involved in the marriage ceremony.

A CEREMONY TO REMEMBER WORKSHEET

Ceremony

Ceremony Site: _____

Address: _____

_____

Date: _____ Time: _____

Contact person at ceremony site: _____

Phone: _____ Fax: _____

Cost: _____

Officiant Name: _____

Processional Decisions

_____

_____

_____

_____

Processional Order

Names of attendants in order of appearance:

_____	_____
_____	_____
_____	_____
_____	_____
_____	_____
_____	_____
_____	_____
_____	_____
_____	_____
_____	_____
_____	_____
_____	_____

Bride's Entrance & Escort: _____

Special Gestures: _____

Escorted by: _____

Readings/Prayers

Reader Name: _____

Selected reading: _____

Reader Name: _____

Selected reading: _____

Reader Name: _____

Selected reading: _____

Bride's Vows (special wordings, verses): _____
_____
_____
_____
_____

Groom's Vows (special wordings, verses): _____
_____
_____
_____
_____

Ring exchange (special requests): _____
_____
_____
_____

Final Blessing/Benediction: _____
_____
_____
_____
_____

Recessional

Names in reverse order:

_____   _____
_____   _____
_____   _____
_____   _____
_____   _____
_____   _____
_____   _____
_____   _____
_____   _____
_____   _____

Special gestures or inclusions: _____
_____
_____
_____
_____
_____

WHAT TO LOOK FOR IN THIS CHAPTER:

- The golden rules of reception planning.

- What to ask your caterer.

- 3 Parts of the reception: cocktail reception, dinner reception, cutting of the cake.

- Guest book options.

- Hassle free seating arrangements.

- Toasting the bride and groom.

- From the first dance to the last dance, and the dances in between.

- Favors—to be or not to be?

- The cake cutting ceremony.

- Tossing the bouquet and removing the garter.

- Exiting the reception as Mr. and Mrs.

- Reception blueprint worksheets.

Your Reception Blueprint

8

> *It's crucial that the bride and groom have absolute confidence in the competency level of the catering facility. The bride does not need the added burden of being the director of her own wedding on her big day. Choose a caterer who is experienced, trustworthy, and one who will give you the ultimate in personal service.*
>
> —David Chase, Director of Catering
> Ritz Carlton New York at Battery Park, NY
> www.ritzcarlton.com

No less important is the wedding's finale: the reception. By the turn of the twentieth century, the social setting for weddings outgrew the intimacy of private homes and moved into hotels, a trend popularized by the vastly wealthy Rockefeller and Vanderbilt families.

As hotels became more opulent so did the desire to entertain in them. A hotel wedding reception began as a luxury reserved for the wealthy, but as banquet facilities cropped up in less expensive hotels, it became the standard for entertaining that we see today.

Just as your wedding dress is probably the most expensive dress you will own, your wedding reception is probably the most expensive party you will ever host. Weddings are special, so afford yourself the time necessary to make your day memorable. Here are some specifics to consider before you book your wedding reception site. These tips apply to any reception. A small wedding does not necessarily mean a casual wedding reception. Even if you opt for a sailboat wedding with two guests, make it memorable.

THE GOLDEN RULES OF PLANNING YOUR RECEPTION

"When are you getting married?" "How many?" These are the questions you will be asked as soon as you call to book your reception. Start by introducing yourself, and tell them you are checking for availability. Booking a reception can be a challenge and you want to inquire respectfully in order to be afforded respect. You'll want a good relationship with your facility from the start. If they seem cold or uninterested in your patronage, move on. This is a joyous occasion, not a chore.

1. Plan your ceremony and reception sites within a reasonable distance.

Location, location, location. Plan your reception within a reasonable distance of your ceremony. For example, if your ceremony is at a church, synagogue, temple, etc. chances are great there is a catering facility within it. Is it an acceptable location for your reception? If the answer is no, look in the vicinity for other possibilities. Try to keep the ceremony and reception located within a twenty-five minute drive.

For sentimental reasons, one bride wanted to get married at her childhood church located 40 miles from her home. She then selected a reception site near her home so she could extend the partying. As her wedding day approached the weather forecast called for heavy rain. Unwilling and unable to change her plans the bride showed up at the church in a torrential downpour. As the ceremony commenced, the rain worsened. By the time she and the groom got to the reception roadways were flooding. The storm escalated to near hurricane proportions. Needless to say, the reception was a huge disappointment because many guests never made it. The bride never got over that rainy day.

2. Book immediately.

Choose your reception site early. Many couples determine their wedding date based on the availability of the reception site. Because so many couples wish to marry on a weekend, facilities can be booked more than a year in advance. If you have your heart set on a specific reception site book it immediately upon your engagement. Another option is to marry during the week. Wednesday or Thursday are favored days.

3. Choose a location that accomodates your guests.

Make sure you comfortably accommodate the number of guests invited to your reception. If you have 125 guests it is unwise to choose a place the size of a football stadium. On the other hand if you have 250 guests don't stuff them into a room that has a capacity of 200. It's against fire laws anyway!

4. Read and understand what your contract says.

Ask for a contract spelling out exactly what you have agreed to with the catering facility. Make sure you have a breakdown of each service you are contracting. For instance, if your caterer supplies linens and floral arrangements get those quotes itemized in the contract. Find out the deposit required to reserve the space—usually about 50%.

Ask to read the cancellation clause in the contract, in the event your wedding is cancelled. Find out about the refund policy of your deposit.

5. Get all the facts.

Qualify your reception site with the Chamber of Commerce or the Better

Business Bureau. Chances are your site is familiar to you or it was personally recommended. In any case, take the contract home and review it thoroughly. Before you sign it make sure all your questions are answered.

6. Don't go over your budget.

Stay within your budget. The average cost of a U.S. wedding is $19,000. Most couples contribute anywhere from 10% to 50% of the cost. The most expensive part of the wedding is the reception. If it looks like you are going over budget, work with your caterer to come up with revisions *before* you sign the contract.

THE CATERER

Here is a checklist of questions to ask your caterer before you book the site.

1. What is the maximum occupancy of the site? For a buffet? For a seated dinner?
2. What is the rental fee of the site and for how many hours? Is there an overtime fee? Can you arrange for more time at the end of the reception if it's going well, or do you have to arrange it beforehand?
3. Does the site provide adequate parking? How much is it and who is charged?
4. What are the charges for doormen, valet parking attendants, coat-check and restroom attendants? From tents to toilets what are the rental fees?
5. How many other events are planned that day? How can you protect your privacy?
6. Will the banquet manager or head caterer be present during your reception?
7. Is there a changing room for the bride and bridal party separate from the public restrooms?
8. Where can a receiving line be set up at the reception site?
9. Is there an ante room where guests can enjoy a cocktail reception before the main course?
10. Are there any hidden costs such as furniture or appliance rental fees? Is a security deposit required?

Make sure all service people have each other's phone numbers, from the banquet manager to the DJ/band to the baker and florist. It will be easier on you if they contact one another directly rather than using you as the middleman. Appoint someone to answer questions that come up during the reception to avoid spending the evening resolving conflicts when you would rather be partying with your guests.

A BLUEPRINT

Now that you have decided on the reception site you are ready for the next chunk of planning. Don't start decorating before you know how the room can be set up to accommodate your guests. Ask for a room layout or blueprint. Copy it and "design" where you, your bridal party, your family and guests will sit. Will you have round tables or banquet tables? Round tables create a more intimate setting but banquet

Ask for a room layout.

tables seat more people. How many tables will you need? How many people can you seat at each table? Does the cook require a meal matched with a name or a general count of each choice?

If they need to match the meal to the guest your response cards will need to be worded appropriately. If a family of four responds with two beef and two fish, but the servers need to know who is eating which, you'll need cards that indicate that.

Do you want a sit-down dinner or a buffet reception? Buffets generally cost more because more food is prepared. A sit-down dinner has a set menu.

COCKTAIL HOUR

Don't miss your cocktail reception. Most wedding receptions take place in three parts: cocktail reception, dinner reception, cutting the cake. The cocktail reception gives everyone a chance to make the transition from solemnity of the ceremony to party time. It is a wonderful time to receive your guests if you have not done so at your ceremony site.

Another feature of the cocktail hour is that it allows you and the groom more time for formal photographs; however, you don't want to miss your reception due to an unduly long period with photos. Your banquet manager will be concerned about serving the meal at its best and you will want some time with your guests, so be sure to keep a good pace between ceremony and reception. Plan to have the large group shots done with your families immediately after the wedding. Smaller group shots can be arranged during the reception.

COCKTAIL HOUR TABOOS

1. Don't arrive so late at your cocktail reception that you are unable to enjoy it. After all, you want to be a part of all you've planned.
2. Don't allow too much time to lapse between your ceremony and reception. In general allow no more than 90 minutes between the two. If you must have more time, arrange a pre-reception where guests can congregate for light non-alcoholic beverages and snacks.
3. Don't drink alcohol on an empty stomach. Be sure you eat something before your ceremony and watch your alcoholic intake during your cocktail reception.

THE GUEST BOOK

Most of the time couples enjoy having a guest book where guests sign their name and perhaps include a message. A guest book can be placed on the table along with the place cards. A simple classic guest book will do, however, some couples are opting for other ideas.

One California couple had a casual photo taken, and displayed it in the center of a picture frame. Around the photo was a large canvas so all guests could write their name and share a message. The couple then had it mounted and framed for display in their home.

DINNER RECEPTION

You and your caterer can create a menu that will satisfy your guests, based on your budget. This brings us to another integral part of the reception: the seating plan. This will take considerable time and juggling so start this project when you have received all your response cards. In general, seat people with others of similar interests. A table of young people or single people will be fun. If parents are divorced seat them away from each other. Seat married couples together as well as singles with escorts. Stuck on where to seat the "extras"? Determine who the extroverts are and have them "head" a table. They will start conversations and introduce everyone to each other.

SEATING

Paper Cutouts

One of the best ways to sort out a seating chart is to make paper cutouts of tables and placement cards. Cut out the number of tables you need for your reception. Cut small place cards with each guest's name on it. Keep shuffling the names from one table to another until you have a suitable seating arrangement. This task is notoriously frustrating, so ask for help and keep your cool. When you've succeeded, you are ready to make up permanent table cards and/or place cards.

> Seat your guests with ease and grace and avoid the seating nightmare.

Table Cards

Each guest needs a card indicating the table at which he/she will sit. Write the first and last name of the guest on the card along with the table number you have assigned. (Ex: Jean Smith – Table 4.) Have each card placed on a table near the entrance of the reception room and arrange each one in alphabetical order.

Place Cards

If the wedding is very formal individual place cards at each place setting are appropriate. Use tent cards and write each guest's name on front and back. This will assure that everyone at the table will know each other - by name. For creative place card ideas see the section on *Wedding Favors*. (page 100.)

Place Cards for the Bridal Party and Parents' Table

Write cards for everyone in your bridal party and both parents' tables. The bride and groom sit in the center of the room (groom on the bride's left) flanked by the best man (seated next to the bride) and the maid/matron of honor (seated next to the groom). Seat all other bridesmaids and ushers alternately. At the parents' tables seat them opposite each other so they can host the tables. In cases of larger families you may consider seating each parent at different tables. Be sure to include your officiant and guest at a prominent table.

TOASTING

Toasting became a fashionable sport during 16th century France as gentlemen toasted all ladies present at a dinner to express their adoration. A formal toast at weddings has become a traditional gesture to wish good luck to the bride and groom. The formal toast is given when everyone is seated, prior to food service. The first person to offer the toast is usually the best man. He explains his relationship to the bride and groom and then toasts to their "everlasting happiness."

Other toasts may follow from the groom, the bride and her maid/matron of honor if warranted. A British tradition has the groom stand to thank the bride's parents for hosting and all the guests for coming by beginning his speech with the words, "My wife and I...," generating cheers from the crowd for his first formal use of the title.

The favored beverage is champagne, but fruit punch, sparkling cider or apple juice is also festive. When you are being toasted you don't drink, just as when being honored you do not applaud yourself. Once the toasting has abated, the best man can read congratulatory telegrams from loved ones.

DANCING

A festive custom at weddings is the first dance. Begin the dancing early and often if you and your groom enjoy dancing. You and the groom start the evening off—the first dance as husband and wife. Ask your bandleader or DJ to announce you and choose a favorite piece of music to dance to. You can dance a few steps with your husband and then change partners. The next dance is with the bride and her father while the groom dances with his mother. Your next partner is the best man while the groom dances with the maid/matron of honor. Finally it's time for your new in-laws.

The bride dances with her father-in-law, while the groom twirls the mother-of-the-bride. Dancing customs are optional. If other scenarios are more suitable forget about tradition and create your own.

Many brides are surprised to learn how fragile their wedding gowns are when they are on the dance floor. As the dancing heats up the chances of severe "injury" to a bridal gown increase. On many occasions gowns are ripped, torn and completely ruined because the dancing gets raucous. Your wedding day is a day of festivity but remember that dancing the night away doesn't mean doing swan dives across the dance floor.

FAVORS

The jury is out as to whether or not wedding favors for the guests should be included at the wedding. In many cases it becomes a matter of budget. For some it is a matter of detail. If wedding favors are definitely desired, consider the many choices available to you. Magazines and websites show abundant ideas for wedding favors in all price ranges. You can even get prepackaged chocolates, ribbons and all, from sites for gift companies, such as **www.chocolatecheers.com** or champagne splits from **www.pop-champagne.com**.

Whether you choose candles, silver or miniature flowerpots decide where you want the favors displayed. Some brides prefer to place the favors at each table place setting. Some choose to place the favors on a separate table to be taken as each guest leaves the wedding. Still others find a way to double the use of favors as unique place cards. Depending on the location and style of your wedding you may find a favor that will be the perfect tie-in. For a beach wedding, sand dollars can make cute favors. Miniature silver frames can serve as place cards and wedding favors for a formal wedding. Be creative and look into unlikely sources for ideas.

One bride decided to create sugar cookies shaped like butterflies and turn them into place cards. The cookies were mounted on different length sticks, wrapped in cellophane and tied with a ribbon and tag with each guest's name and table number on it. The "butterflies" were then stuck in pots of wheat grass. Because the sticks were varying lengths, the butterflies created a beautiful flying spectacle for guests arriving at the reception. After all, the first impression of your reception room will be a lasting one!

Clever edible place cards come with a caveat, according to JoAnn Gregoli owner of *Elegant Occasions* in Denville, NJ. She used large chocolates shaped like Hershey's Kisses that were foil-wrapped. The "flags" on each chocolate had the seating assignment written on it. Unfortunately, many guests ate the chocolates and threw away their seating assignments not realizing the dual purpose of the wedding favors.

CUTTING THE CAKE

Have a quick rehearsal with your fiance' so you both know where to stand and how to hold the knife, so that your photographer can get a good angle | Cake in the face is a no no. | while still leaving an open view for your guests. It's a surprisingly precise little ceremony if you don't pay attention to what you have to do. The groom and bride share the handle while cutting a single slice. They take turns feeding one another, gently, and then it is whisked away by wait staff to be served to the guests. (Please, no cake in the face.)

One couple was unprepared for the density of their cake and could not get the knife through it. Flustered they leaned in to push harder, prompting the photographer to interrupt and reposition them. When they did make the cut, the entire tier pulled up from the one below it. Luckily, they were able to laugh it off and finally removed a slice. Unfortunately, they didn't know who to feed first. Luckily the awkwardness made some of the most charming photographs later.

Such unrehearsed moments are destined to occur, but try to minimize the possibility that they will, by thinking of the little moments as well as the big ones. Too much confusion will make the wedding seem sloppy.

TOSSING THE BOUQUET

After the cutting of the cake you may want to include the traditional bridal toss and the removal of the garter. These are optional but fun if you both are in agreement, and willing to do it tastefully. There is no hard and fast rule that *The Stripper* be played during garter removal, and some of the most elegant garters can be found at ***www.PerfectDetails.com***.

Tossing the bridal bouquet traditionally meant that the maid who caught it was the next bride-to-be. Have a separate bouquet made if you don't want yours ruined. Choose a staircase or balcony where you can do a backward toss. You may ask the band or DJ to play some catchy music or ask for a drum roll.

REMOVING THE GARTER

Now it's his turn. The groom removes the garter from the bride's leg accompanied by fun music or a drum roll. Then he tosses it to the other bachelors in the room. The one who catches it gets to put it on the leg of the maid who caught the bouquet. This is a lot of fun but there are times this "ceremony" can become inappropriate. Keep it clean. You don't want an embarrassing moment to tarnish your beautiful day.

EXITING THE RECEPTION

As the guests of honor you will want to exit your reception just as you entered, in grand style. Be sure you say a special goodbye and thank-you to your parents and loved ones before you leave the reception. Dance your last dance to a favorite music choice, then make your exit graciously and gracefully as your guests shower you with best wishes and confetti of your choice.

Exit your reception in grand style.

You will have predetermined what mode of transportation you will use to leave your reception. Is it in a limousine, a classic car, horse-drawn carriage, maybe a motorcycle or bicycle? You decide…and have fun from this day forward!

YOUR RECEPTION BLUEPRINT WORKSHEET

INDOOR RECEPTION WORKSHEET

Name of Reception Site: _____

Address: _____

Phone: _____ Fax: _____ E-mail: _____

Contact person: _____

Total estimated cost: $_____

Overtime fee: _____ per hour

Facility provisions

Room capacity: _____

Seated dinner: _____

Buffet reception: _____

Cocktail reception area: _____

Receiving line area: _____

Food

Hors d'oeuvres:_____

Food stations: _____

Salads: _____

Main course: _____

Special dishes: _____

Ethnic foods: _____

Desserts: _____

Wedding cake: _____

Total Estimated Cost: $_____

Beverages

Champagne: _____ toast only _____ open service _____

Wine (white): _____ open service _____ dinner only _____

Wine (red): _____ open service _____ dinner only _____

Full bar set-up:_____ open service _____ hours from ___ to ___

Non-alcoholic beverages: _____

        Juices _____

        Punch _____

        Tea/coffee _____

After dinner liqueurs: $_____

Total Estimated Cost: $_____

Waiter/Bartender Service

of wait staff: _____

hours from: _____ to _____

overtime fee: _____

Est. Cost: $_____

Miscellaneous

Valet Parking attendants: _____ cost _____

Reserved Parking Lot: _____ cost _____

Coat Check Attendants: _____ cost _____

Restroom Attendants: _____ cost _____

Changing Room: _____ cost _____

Other requests: _____ cost _____

Cake supplied: yes _____ no _____ cost _____

Flowers/décor: yes _____ no _____ cost _____

DJ/band: yes _____ no _____ cost _____

Photographer: yes _____ no _____ cost _____

Videographer: yes _____ no _____ cost _____

Transportation: yes _____ no _____ cost _____

Other provisions: yes _____ no _____ cost _____

Date contract signed: _____

Final guest count deadline: _____

Deposit paid/date: _____

Final deadline for special services: _____

Balance due/date: _____

OUTDOOR RECEPTION

You will need all catering services outlined for an indoor reception plus additional rental equipment.

Rental Site
Name: _____
Address: _____
Phone: _____ Fax: _____ E-mail: _____
Contact person: _____
Contract signed: _____ Deposit/date: _____
Balance due/date: _____
Total cost: _____

Rental Company:
Name: _____
Address: _____
Phone: _____ Fax: _____ E-mail: _____
Contact person: _____
Contract signed: _____ Deposit/date: _____
Balance due/date: _____
Total cost: _____

Caterer (follow outline for indoor reception)
Name: _____
Address: _____
Phone: _____ Fax: _____ E-mail: _____
Contact person: _____
Contract signed: _____ Deposit/date: _____
Balance due/date: _____
Total cost: _____

Equipment:
Chairs: _____ cost _____
Tables: _____ cost _____
Dance floor: _____ cost _____
Lights: _____ cost _____
Linens: _____ cost _____
Tableware: _____ cost _____
Tent: _____ cost _____
Add'l tents/tables: _____ cost _____
Power generator: _____ cost _____
Portable potties: _____ cost _____
Other: _____ cost _____
Total Equipment Cost: $ _____

ADDITIONAL NOTES:

ADDITIONAL NOTES:

WHAT TO LOOK FOR IN THIS CHAPTER:

- The wedding stationery you select represents your wedding style.

- Consult experts for proper wording and etiquette.

- Be sure to weigh your invitation plus enclosures for adequate postage.

- Consider clever ways to enhance simple cardstock invitations for an upscale look.

- Worksheet order forms for stationery.

- Wedding guest list forms (copy what you need).

- Out-of-town guest forms (copy what you need).

- Attach response cards to guest list forms for convenience.

9 STATIONERY WITH STYLE

> *"More than just exemplify your wedding's style, your stationery invites, guides, and informs."*
> -Bonnie Siegel Marcus
> Product Manager, NY, NY
> www.chelseapaper.com

Your wedding invitations set the tone for the wedding and give the guests a glimpse of what to expect. Is your wedding traditional? Chances are you will select traditional wedding stationery. If your taste is contemporary then your invitation will most likely have a contemporary look to it. The more formal the wedding the more you will want to honor wedding stationery protocol. If your wedding is informal a simple invitation is perfectly acceptable.

Let your stationery reflect the style of your wedding.

By now you should know your wedding style, time, date and place. Perhaps most importantly, you are now well acquainted with your budget. The next step is to determine your guest list, order the invitations, and determine how much stationery you will need. Following is a breakdown of stationery necessities and accessories. For an in-depth guide to wedding stationery and etiquette consult companies such as *www.chelseapaper.com*.

WEDDING INVITATIONS

Order more than you need for keepsakes, last minute guests, and accidents. Your RSVP (a French phrase, literally translated means "respond if you please") should be dated at least two weeks prior to your wedding, or according to your reception hall's deadline. Verify the date of the RSVP with your caterer. Your invitation is completely spelled out including times, dates, numbers, addresses and churches/temples. Be sure to include the letter "u" in the spelling of "honour"—if your wedding is formal and religious.

Refer to professional stationery for wording and multiple options.

"Honour of your presence" is used if you are being married in a house of worship. If not, "pleasure of your company" is appropriate. Determine if the groom's parents will be listed on the invitation. Use your first name, omitting your surname unless it is different from your parents (you were married once before) or your wedding is being sponsored/hosted by someone other than your parents (a relative, friend or associate). If you, your fiancé or one of your parents has a professional title use it and spell it in full unless space does not permit.

RESPONSE CARDS

Traditionally response cards were not included in the invitation but modern brides find response cards a great convenience. These cards validate your guest list and provide an easy way to keep track of your head count. Many brides file them in a card file box and write notes on them regarding gifts, arrival times, and special needs, etc. Some banquet halls want to know exactly who is eating what so their wait staff can deliver each meal by referencing your guest's place-card. If so, your response card will have to be worded accordingly.

Response cards allow you to manage the guest count.

The typical response card reads:

> The favor of a reply is requested by the first of June 1.
> M _____ will _____ attend.

If you are inviting families write out each name of the family member on the interior invitation envelope. If children are not invited, list only the parents' name on the envelope.

If you want to encourage a traditional response the card reads:

> The favor of a reply is requested.

The guest should reply by writing out:

> Mr. and Mrs. James Lacey
> accept the kind invitation
> at the marriage of their daughter
> on Saturday, June 1
> at 6:00 PM

Consider whether the invitation will include maps and directions. Traditionally it should stand by itself. Consider postage costs. Will it be easier to include all information at once, or is it feasible to do a separate mailing? Always have a complete invitation weighed at the post office before mailing to your whole list. Insufficient postage will create a slew of problems. Send all invitations at the same time. Decide if you want a calligrapher to hand address invitations.

Carefully determine what enclosures your guests need.

When choosing your style of invitation, ask your stationery store if you can bring their sample book home. An evening spent perusing invitation styles will give you a chance to weigh your many choices. Chances are, you will find a decoration that provides your guests with an image of your wedding in advance. An autumn wedding invitation may arrive at their home in mid-August, but gold lettering and a leaf motif will put them in the mood for an embracing colorful ceremony that fall. Handmade invitations can be very costly but ideal for an exclusive wedding. Consider *www.idoinvitations.com*. For more cost effective invitations, look into elegant cardstock with beautiful lettering and "do it yourself" decorative flowers, leaves, feathers, etc.

While choosing a reception site calls for serious thought, the invitation is an area where your personality can shine through. It's a good way to get the ball rolling toward your big day and is often the step that makes your wedding start to feel real.

Mr. and Mrs. Lawson Andrew James

request the honour of your presence

at the marriage of their daughter

Sarah Louise

to

Mr. Richard Cole Thorton

Saturday, the fifth of June

The year two thousand

at six o'clock

Church of Saint Michael

Little Rock, Arkansas

A sample of a formal invitation (courtesy of chelseapaper.com)

Please share our happiness
in celebration of our marriage
Monday, the fourth of September
Two thousand
at eleven o'clock in the morning
Eagle's Nest
Vail, Colorado

Lani Pilch and Bill Silvers

Please join us following the ceremony
for Luncheon and Dancing

A sample of an informal invitation (courtesy of chelseapaper.com)

STATIONERY WITH STYLE WORKSHEET

Name of Vendor: _____

Address: _____

_____

Phone: _____ Fax: _____ Website: _____

Contact: _____

ENGAGEMENT ANNOUNCEMENTS

	Amount Ordered	Date Ordered	Date Received	Date Sent	Cost
Save-the-date cards					
Engagement Party Invitations					
Bridal Shower Invitations					
Bachelor Party Invitations					
Bachelorette Party Invitations					

WEDDING INVITATIONS

	Amount Ordered	Date Ordered	Date Received	Date Sent	Cost
Invitations					
Reception Cards					
Response Cards					
Within-the-Ribbon Cards					
Directional Cards					
At Home Cards					

THANK-YOU NOTES

	Amount Ordered	Date Ordered	Date Received	Date Sent	Cost
Couple's					
His					
Hers					

OTHER STATIONERY

	Amount Ordered	Date Ordered	Date Received	Date Sent	Cost
Weekend Wedding Destination Cards					
Rain Date Cards					
Programs					
Napkins					
Matchbooks					
Other					

Stationery With Style

WEDDING GUEST LIST

Guest Name: _____

Address: _____

Phone: _____ Fax: _____ E-mail: _____

Children's names: _____

_____

Wedding/Reception invitation sent: _____ Date: _____

    Attending _____ Not attending _____ Wedding Announcement Only_____

\# of Attendees: _____

Engagement Gift: _____ Date Thank-you Sent: _____

Shower Gift: _____ Date Thank-you Sent: _____

Wedding Gift: _____ Date Thank-you Sent: _____

                    ❧   ❧   ❧

Guest Name: _____

Address: _____

Phone: _____ Fax: _____ E-mail: _____

Children's names: _____

_____

Wedding/Reception invitation sent: _____ Date: _____

    Attending _____ Not attending _____ Wedding Announcement Only_____

\# of Attendees: _____

Engagement Gift: _____ Date Thank-you Sent: _____

Shower Gift: _____ Date Thank-you Sent: _____

Wedding Gift: _____ Date Thank-you Sent: _____

                    ❧   ❧   ❧

Guest Name: _____

Address: _____

Phone: _____ Fax: _____ E-mail: _____

Children's names: _____

_____

Wedding/Reception invitation sent: _____ Date: _____

    Attending _____ Not attending _____ Wedding Announcement Only_____

\# of Attendees: _____

Engagement Gift: _____ Date Thank-you Sent: _____

Shower Gift: _____ Date Thank-you Sent: _____

Wedding Gift: _____ Date Thank-you Sent: _____

Guest Name: _____

Address: _____

Phone: _____ Fax: _____ E-mail: _____

Children's names: _____

_____

Wedding/Reception invitation sent: _____ Date: _____

   Attending _____ Not attending _____ Wedding Announcement Only_____

# of Attendees: _____

Engagement Gift: _____ Date Thank-you Sent: _____

Shower Gift: _____ Date Thank-you Sent: _____

Wedding Gift: _____ Date Thank-you Sent: _____

              ❧   ❧   ❧

Guest Name: _____

Address: _____

Phone: _____ Fax: _____ E-mail: _____

Children's names: _____

_____

Wedding/Reception invitation sent: _____ Date: _____

   Attending _____ Not attending _____ Wedding Announcement Only_____

# of Attendees: _____

Engagement Gift: _____ Date Thank-you Sent: _____

Shower Gift: _____ Date Thank-you Sent: _____

Wedding Gift: _____ Date Thank-you Sent: _____

              ❧   ❧   ❧

Guest Name: _____

Address: _____

Phone: _____ Fax: _____ E-mail: _____

Children's names: _____

_____

Wedding/Reception invitation sent: _____ Date: _____

   Attending _____ Not attending _____ Wedding Announcement Only_____

# of Attendees: _____

Engagement Gift: _____ Date Thank-you Sent: _____

Shower Gift: _____ Date Thank-you Sent: _____

Wedding Gift: _____ Date Thank-you Sent: _____

Guest Name: _____

Address: _____

Phone: _____ Fax: _____ E-mail: _____

Children's names: _____

_____

Wedding/Reception invitation sent: _____ Date: _____

Attending _____ Not attending _____ Wedding Announcement Only_____

# of Attendees: _____

Engagement Gift: _____ Date Thank-you Sent: _____

Shower Gift: _____ Date Thank-you Sent: _____

Wedding Gift: _____ Date Thank-you Sent: _____

❧   ❧   ❧

Guest Name: _____

Address: _____

Phone: _____ Fax: _____ E-mail: _____

Children's names: _____

_____

Wedding/Reception invitation sent: _____ Date: _____

Attending _____ Not attending _____ Wedding Announcement Only_____

# of Attendees: _____

Engagement Gift: _____ Date Thank-you Sent: _____

Shower Gift: _____ Date Thank-you Sent: _____

Wedding Gift: _____ Date Thank-you Sent: _____

❧   ❧   ❧

Guest Name: _____

Address: _____

Phone: _____ Fax: _____ E-mail: _____

Children's names: _____

_____

Wedding/Reception invitation sent: _____ Date: _____

Attending _____ Not attending _____ Wedding Announcement Only_____

# of Attendees: _____

Engagement Gift: _____ Date Thank-you Sent: _____

Shower Gift: _____ Date Thank-you Sent: _____

Wedding Gift: _____ Date Thank-you Sent: _____

WEDDING GUEST LIST

Stationery With Style

Guest Name: _____

Address: _____

Phone: _____ Fax: _____ E-mail: _____

Children's names: _____

_____

Wedding/Reception invitation sent: _____ Date: _____

Attending _____ Not attending _____ Wedding Announcement Only _____

# of Attendees: _____

Engagement Gift: _____ Date Thank-you Sent: _____

Shower Gift: _____ Date Thank-you Sent: _____

Wedding Gift: _____ Date Thank-you Sent: _____

         ❧ ❧ ❧

Guest Name: _____

Address: _____

Phone: _____ Fax: _____ E-mail: _____

Children's names: _____

_____

Wedding/Reception invitation sent: _____ Date: _____

Attending _____ Not attending _____ Wedding Announcement Only _____

# of Attendees: _____

Engagement Gift: _____ Date Thank-you Sent: _____

Shower Gift: _____ Date Thank-you Sent: _____

Wedding Gift: _____ Date Thank-you Sent: _____

         ❧ ❧ ❧

Guest Name: _____

Address: _____

Phone: _____ Fax: _____ E-mail: _____

Children's names: _____

_____

Wedding/Reception invitation sent: _____ Date: _____

Attending _____ Not attending _____ Wedding Announcement Only _____

# of Attendees: _____

Engagement Gift: _____ Date Thank-you Sent: _____

Shower Gift: _____ Date Thank-you Sent: _____

Wedding Gift: _____ Date Thank-you Sent: _____

WEDDING GUEST LIST

Stationery With Style

ACCOMMODATIONS FOR OUT-OF-TOWN GUESTS

(Photocopy what you need for tracking out-of town guests. Cut into thirds and attach to guest list information.)

Guest Name: _____ # of Family Members: _____

Address: _____

Phone: _____ Fax: _____ E-mail: _____

Arrival Date: _____ Arriving by (flight #, train, etc.):_____

Departure Date: _____ Time: _____

Accommodations at: _____

Address: _____

Transportation Needs to Wedding: _____

Other Transportation Needs: _____

Childcare Needs: _____

Additional Needs (dietary, handicap, etc.): _____

Attending Rehearsal Dinner: Yes   No

❧   ❧   ❧

Guest Name: _____ # of Family Members: _____

Address: _____

Phone: _____ Fax: _____ Email: _____

Arrival Date: _____ Arriving by (flight #, train, etc.):_____

Departure Date: _____ Time: _____

Accommodations at: _____

Address: _____

Transportation Needs to Wedding: _____

Other Transportation Needs: _____

Childcare Needs: _____

Additional Needs (dietary, handicap, etc.): _____

Attending Rehearsal Dinner: Yes   No

❧   ❧   ❧

Guest Name: _____ # of Family Members: _____

Address: _____

Phone: _____ Fax: _____ E-mail: _____

Arrival Date: _____ Arriving by (flight #, train, etc.):_____

Departure Date: _____ Time: _____

Accommodations at: _____

Address: _____

Transportation Needs to Wedding: _____

Other Transportation Needs: _____

Childcare Needs: _____

Additional Needs (dietary, handicap, etc.): _____

Attending Rehearsal Dinner: Yes   No

Guest Name: _____ # of Family Members: _____
Address: _____
Phone: _____ Fax: _____ E-mail: _____
Arrival Date: _____ Arriving by (flight #, train, etc.):_____
Departure Date: _____ Time: _____
Accommodations at: _____
Address: _____

_____

Transportation Needs to Wedding: _____
Other Transportation Needs: _____
Childcare Needs: _____
Additional Needs (dietary, handicap, etc.): _____
Attending Rehearsal Dinner: Yes   No

&a   &a   &a

Guest Name: _____ # of Family Members: _____
Address: _____
Phone: _____ Fax: _____ E-mail: _____
Arrival Date: _____ Arriving by (flight #, train, etc.):_____
Departure Date: _____ Time: _____
Accommodations at: _____
Address: _____

_____

Transportation Needs to Wedding: _____
Other Transportation Needs: _____
Childcare Needs: _____
Additional Needs (dietary, handicap, etc.): _____
Attending Rehearsal Dinner: Yes   No

&a   &a   &a

Guest Name: _____ # of Family Members: _____
Address: _____
Phone: _____ Fax: _____ E-mail: _____
Arrival Date: _____ Arriving by (flight #, train, etc.):_____
Departure Date: _____ Time: _____
Accommodations at: _____
Address: _____

_____

Transportation Needs to Wedding: _____
Other Transportation Needs: _____
Childcare Needs: _____
Additional Needs (dietary, handicap, etc.): _____
Attending Rehearsal Dinner: Yes   No

OUT-OF-TOWN GUEST LIST

Stationery With Style

WHAT TO LOOK FOR IN THIS CHAPTER:

- Set the tone for your wedding with music.

- 4 music parts to the ceremony—prelude, processional, recessional, postlude.

- Finding the right musicians or recordings.

- Hiring musicians, DJs and/or equipment.

- Reception Music—tips to follow before you make your final decision.

- Ceremony music tips that make perfect harmony.

- Estimate worksheets for music at the reception.

- Ceremony musical selections from prelude to postlude.

- Reception musical selections from receiving line to last dance.

10
Music, Music, Music

> A good band is like a good team of doctors. They diagnose the audience, prescribe the perfect mix of music, and monitor the pacing for an unforgettable event.
>
> —Bernie Leiner, Owner
> Harbor Lights Music, Westchester, NY
> www.harborlightsmusic.com

Long after the flowers have wilted, the food has been consumed, guests will remember if they had a good time at a wedding. Music is high on the list of what guests remember most about weddings. If the music is good, they recall a wonderful time. If the music is too loud, they remember that. If the music is bland they remember the wedding as dull. Music helps set the tone and style of your wedding yet many brides spend entirely too much time determining the music at their reception and ignoring the music at the ceremony. Both are important and command equal attention.

CEREMONY

From the first downbeat, music sets the mood of your wedding.

Music at your wedding ceremony consists of four parts: the **prelude**, the **processional**, the **recessional**, and the **postlude**. The prelude music begins 15 to 30 minutes before the ceremony while guests are being seated.

No bride can manage to be present during the prelude music if she wants to make a grand entrance. In one instance, the bride coordinated the prelude music between the organist and/or other musician, intending them to play alternately. Apparently her instructions did not get through to the organist, who played nothing—leaving the other musician to play, play, play. To make matters worse, the bride was late arriving to the ceremony, and the other musician was a bagpiper who was completely exhausted from playing continuously. Worse yet, he couldn't leave his location at the front of the church to speak to the organist in the choir loft. By the time the bride arrived, the guests' ears were shattered from the shrill overtones of the piper. This was one time the bride wished she had hired a wedding consultant for the day, to march up to the organist and get him playing.

You may decide on interim musical selections during the ceremony particularly if you are lighting unity candles or want some "breathing room" between readings or prayers. You must ask your officiant if secular music (non-religious) is permitted at your house of worship. Some religions have strict rules governing the type of music (if any) that can be performed. Needless to say you don't want a disaster like the aforementioned bride's.

PROCESSIONAL & RECESSIONAL MUSIC

The **processional** music begins when the first member of the bridal party walks down the aisle. The **recessional** music starts when the bride and groom exit the "altar" as husband and wife. Finally the **postlude** music is played as your guests exit the ceremony site.

MUSIC SELECTIONS

Consider unique instrumental choices.

The music you select depends on the style of wedding you are having. Traditional music works well with a traditional setting and style. If you opt for a less conservative wedding you may select more modern music in keeping with the style. Organ music is an easy choice because most worship houses own organs, but other instrumentation is a wonderful variation on the norm. Consider a string quartet, a classical guitarist, a harpist, or an instrument that represents a part of your (or his) culture such as a bagpiper, although you may want to keep the piper outdoors if the church is small. You can also combine organ selections with a trumpet fanfare for your entrance.

FINDING THE RIGHT MUSIC AND HIRING THE MUSICIANS

One couple decided to get married off Cape Cod though they lived in Hawaii. The bride was a Connecticut native and the groom a native Hawaiian. They were married in a traditional Catholic Church setting but the bride had all the flowers including the traditional wedding Hawaiian leis and head wreathes flown to the Cape. The music was a selection of recordings by well-known Hawaiian vocalists. In order to insure a high-end musical quality throughout the church she rented audio equipment and hired a professional to

Don't rule out recorded music.

coordinate the music. Between the music, the fragrant flowers, and the wedding leis and wreaths, the couple created a ceremony that was unique and different. This is the sort of personal touch that demonstrates how much you care, and sets your wedding apart from the rest.

These days you can research a variety of websites to hear musical selections. Try *www.wedalert.com* for your listening pleasure. Many music stores allow you to listen to music while you are shopping. Ask the sales personnel if they have a list of recommended wedding music—many do. Consult your local music directors for musical suggestions and musicians to hire. Ask friends, school personnel and bandleaders for suggestions. Live music adds grace and elegance to a ceremony but if you desire something out of the ordinary recorded music can be pleasant too.

Your ceremony music is the first to be heard by you and your guests. Spend the time to research music that is meaningful so your ceremony is special. Too many wedding ceremonies are "cookie cutters" that lack a personal touch or memorable moment. Music, readings, poems, and cultural customs provide an opportunity for both of you to express yourself. Don't be afraid to incorporate them into your ceremony.

> Avoid the "cookie cutter" ceremony.

THE RECEPTION MUSIC

Now it's party time. Depending on the style of your wedding you have many choices of reception music available to suit your tastes. From traditional to contemporary the music you choose sets the mood and tone. Consider what style of music you want and the size of your reception site. If you choose a band be sure your site accommodates them. A trio in a large hall is lost, whereby a twelve-piece band in a small space is ear splitting. Before you book the musicians ask the caterer what works best in the room. Their experience will guide you to a number of options from which you can choose. Ideally, the more formal your wedding the more advisable it is to have a band or orchestra at your reception. A very formal wedding requires an orchestra.

BAND OR ORCHESTRA

> Swing, rock or waltz?

Is dancing a large part of your wedding or would you rather not dance at all? Most brides and grooms want to dance and therefore choose a band or orchestra that plays musical standards and rock and roll. Trends suggest that more couples are choosing bands that play music from the 1940s featuring swing dancing, foxtrots, tangos, etc. If you and your fiancé love hard rock find a mix that will work well for most of your guests. Lots of couples take dance lessons so they are graceful on the dance floor. Arthur Murray is one to try.

Perhaps neither you nor your husband wants to display your dancing ability, or inability, and prefer good listening music. Your reception can be just as romantic with a wonderful jazz quartet or chamber music ensemble. Ask your caterer for names of bands and check the phonebook, websites and local unions. Ask your friends and find out from other brides who they recommend. Go to bridal fairs and request video and audiotapes. Once you decide on the band or orchestra you want, have a meeting with the bandleader or booking agent. Go over the contract thoroughly.

WHAT ABOUT A DJ?

> Want to hear the real thing? Hire a DJ.

A good DJ can add a spark to your reception and cost far less than a band. If he or she knows their stuff they will not simply play music, they will gauge energy levels and work your crowd accordingly. The advantage is that you can hear a variety of music—waltzes, polkas, mambos or hustles and you can dance to the original recordings. If you decide to hire a DJ write down a selection of tunes you want played during the reception. If you want ethnic music be sure to ask for it in advance so the DJ can have it ready. A good DJ can "pace" your reception so that music flows smoothly through each phase and can be an excellent announcer.

INTRODUCTIONS

"And now for the first time, allow me to present, Mr. and Mrs...."

The DJ or band leader can introduce you and your bridal party as you make your entrance into the reception and introduce your first dance together. The DJ can also help you select which music you want for the cake cutting and garter/bouquet tossing ceremonies. DJs need less performance space than a band and the volume control is more easily controlled. If you are thinking about a DJ for your wedding be sure you interview him or her and ask all the questions you would if you were hiring a band or orchestra. Most importantly make sure they have wedding reception experience.

MUSICAL TIPS TO AVOID A SOUR NOTE

- List your favorite songs.
- Research your sources for a qualified band, orchestra or DJ. Get references and check them out with your local Better Business Bureau.
- Meet with the booking agent, bandleader or DJ before you sign a contract. Determine how many musicians will be present, request particular performers if you consider it important and ask about breaks, set-up time, overtime and special requirements. Ask about food breaks and who will play during them.
- Can the band play special requests and certain ethnic music you want? If you have favorites be sure the band knows them.
- Be specific about which tunes you want played for your first dance, the dance with your father and the groom's dance with his mother. Be specific about the cake cutting music and the garter and bouquet tossing music. Decide what your last dance will be before you exit your reception. Make a list.
- Be sure the band or DJ you hire is familiar with your reception site. If not make an appointment for them to visit the site beforehand. For the reception, ask them to dress in accordance with your wedding style.
- Decide if you want the bandleader or DJ to formally introduce you and your wedding party. Do you want announcements made throughout your reception? If so, what do you want announced?
- Be prepared to pay a 50 percent deposit. Get in writing the number of musicians, the instrumentation and specific performers you want. Include the hours they will perform and get overtime rates in case you want to extend the music. If the band you hired is not the band you get, renegotiate the fee before you pay your balance.

CEREMONY MUSIC TIPS

Follow the tips above for reception music and inquire about music for your ceremony from bandleaders also. Many bandleaders can recommend qualified musicians who can play beautifully for your ceremony. If you have an organist at your ceremony site consider embellishing the music with additional musicians.

> Ceremony music is the first music heard by your guests.

PRELUDE

- Build the music to a crescendo for your entrance.
- Pre-select music for the prelude (choose 4-6 selections) and time them so the total performing time is about 30 minutes. Arrange your selections and have them played in order of preference and importance. Ask the musicians to perform together for one of the selections. Maybe you want a song performed. Mix it up.
- Select the music for your processional. The bridal party processional music can be different from the bride's processional. Consider a fuller instrumentation for the bride's entrance.
- Be sure the soloists know when to perform and where to stand during the ceremony. If they are "on view" be sure they know what to wear. If they use music be sure the music is on a music stand or in a black binder. Make sure they are present at the rehearsal and perform fully.

RECESSIONAL

- Choose your recessional music. Select music that is uplifting and celebratory. Use fuller instrumentation for the newlyweds as you exit. Follow suit for the rest of the bridal party. Keep the music triumphant.

POSTLUDE

- Finally, choose the postlude music. This is a wonderful time for musicians to work together. If you have a string ensemble they can perform a tune with the organist as the guests file. Maybe you have an arrangement for flute and guitar. Arrange the music in order of preference. Depending upon the number of guests figure an average of 10 –15 minutes of postlude music. If all guests have not exited, ask the musicians to continue playing. Be sure the ceremony site is clear of guests before the music stops.
- Be sure you write down all your musical selections for your music coordinator. Make a copy for yourself so you can include the music, composer and performer in your wedding program.
- Be sure to credit musicians in your program.
- Review all fees and additional costs with the music coordinator. If you need to rent audio equipment or instruments include it in your total cost. Tipping is optional but if you decide to tip, 15-20 % is standard.
- Extra tips are appreciated for a job well done.

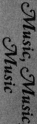

Music, Music, Music

Remember that your musicians, like all of your services, are working for you. Surprisingly, even "professionals" sometimes feel they know better than you, due to their extensive experience. Even the officiant can sometimes lose perspective on your day, having performed many weddings in his or her career. A professional harpist relayed a story to me, of playing *Ave Maria* at a wedding ceremony. She began the piece as she had done hundreds of times before but as she neared the crescendo she noticed the minister motioning for her to stop. She continued to play and again he motioned for her to stop. Apparently the bride and groom had completed a certain ritual and the minister was ready to proceed with the service.

The harpist persisted and again got the motion to stop from the minister. This continued until the harpist caught the eye of the bride who gave her the thumbs-up to finish the piece. The harpist wisely ignored the minister's inappropriate timing and played through the finale. Afterward the bride and groom gratefully thanked her for completing her lovely rendition, which was a cherished moment to them. Had they allowed the minister to stop her, their moment would have been lost over a misunderstanding.

Above all, choose music that you love. If you dance as a couple from the beginning, your friends and family will gladly join you. Even if a dozen things go wrong, it can all be forgotten if everyone dances to their hearts' content.

RECEPTION MUSIC ESTIMATE WORKSHEET

BAND/ORCHESTRA *(Get estimates from multiple bands.)*

Estimate 1

Name of Band/Orchestra: _____

Leader's Name: _____

Address: _____

Phone: _____ Fax: _____ E-mail: _____

\# of Musicians in Band: _____ Will musicians play ceremony?   Yes   No

Style of Music: _____

Music Heard: in person   video/audio tape

Comments on music, style, instrumentation, selections, performers: _____
_____

Name of Referral (if applicable): _____ Phone: _____

Cost of Reception Music: $_____ Cost of Ceremony Music: $_____

Total Cost: $_____

Estimate 2

Name of Band/Orchestra: _____

Leader's Name: _____

Address: _____

Phone: _____ Fax: _____ E-mail: _____

\# of Musicians in Band: _____ Will musicians play ceremony?   Yes   No

Style of Music: _____

Music Heard: in person   video/audio tape

Comments on music, style, instrumentation, selections, performers: _____
_____

Name of Referral (if applicable): _____ Phone: _____

Cost of Reception Music: $_____ Cost of Ceremony Music: $_____

Total Cost: $_____

Estimate 3

Name of Band/Orchestra: _____

Leader's Name: _____

Address: _____

Phone: _____ Fax: _____ E-mail: _____

\# of Musicians in Band: _____ Will musicians play ceremony?   Yes   No

Style of Music: _____

Music Heard: in person   video/audio tape

Comments on music, style, instrumentation, selections, performers: _____
_____

Name of Referral (if applicable): _____ Phone: _____

Cost of Reception Music: $_____ Cost of Ceremony Music: $_____

Total Cost: $_____

Music, Music, Music

FINAL BAND/ORCHESTRA AGREEMENT

Band/Orchestra Selected: _____

\# of Musicians: _____

Particular Soloist Requested: _____

\# of Hours Performing: _____ Beginning at: _____ Ending at: _____

Overtime Rate Per Hour: _____

Play Continuously?   Yes   No

\# of Breaks: _____ Duration of Breaks: _____

Meal Service: Yes   No   How Many: _____

Date Contract Signed: _____ Deposit Amount/Date: _____/_____

Balance Due/Date: _____/_____ Tips: _____

BAND/ORCHESTRA ESTIMATE WORKSHEET

DISC JOCKEY *(Get estimates from multiple DJs.)*

Estimate 1

Name of DJ: _____

Address: _____

Phone: _____ Fax: _____ E-mail _____

Equipment Used: _____

Extra Equipment Required: _____

Special Effects: _____

DJ/Emcee Fee: _____

Spinner Fee: _____

Continuous Music Fee: _____

Overtime Fee: _____

TOTAL COST: _____

Meals: Yes   No

Referred by: _____

Phone: _____

Estimate 2

Name of DJ: _____

Address: _____

Phone: _____ Fax: _____ E-mail: _____

Equipment Used: _____

Extra Equipment Required: _____

Special Effects: _____

DJ/Emcee Fee: _____

Spinner Fee: _____

Continuous Music Fee: _____

Overtime Fee: _____

TOTAL COST: _____

Meals: Yes   No

Referred by: _____

Phone: _____

Music, Music, Music

Estimate 3

Name of DJ: _____

Address: _____

Phone: _____ Fax: _____ E-mail: _____

Equipment Used: _____

Extra Equipment Required: _____

Special Effects: _____

DJ/Emcee Fee: _____

Spinner Fee: _____

Continuous Music Fee: _____

Overtime Fee: _____

TOTAL COST: _____

Meals: Yes   No

Referred by: _____

Phone: _____

ૐ   ૐ   ૐ

FINAL DJ AGREEMENT

Name of DJ: _____

Date Contract Signed: _____ Deposit/Date: _____/_____

Balance Due/Date: _____/_____ Tips: _____

DJ ESTIMATE WORKSHEET

CEREMONY MUSIC SELECTIONS

Prelude (15-30 minutes)

Title	Composer	Performed by
1. _____	_____	_____
2. _____	_____	_____
3. _____	_____	_____
4. _____	_____	_____

Seating of Mothers

1. _____	_____	_____
2. _____	_____	_____

Processional for Wedding Party

_____ _____ _____

Processional for Bride

_____ _____ _____

Music Choices during Ceremony

1. _____	_____	_____
2. _____	_____	_____
3. _____	_____	_____
4. _____	_____	_____

Recessional Music

_____ _____ _____

Postlude Music

1. _____	_____	_____
2. _____	_____	_____
3. _____	_____	_____

Receiving Line Music (personal favorites)

1. _____	_____	_____
2. _____	_____	_____
3. _____	_____	_____

Musical Director/Organist

Name: _____

Address: _____

_____

Phone: _____ Fax: _____ E-mail: _____

Cost: _____

Ensemble Leader

Name: _____ Instrumentation (duo, trio, etc.): _____

Instruments: strings   brass   guitar   piano   harp   flute/woodwind   other

Address: _____

_____

Phone: _____ Fax: _____ E-mail: _____

Cost: _____

Soloist

Name: _____

Address: _____

_____

Phone: _____ Fax: _____ E-mail: _____

Cost: _____

RECEPTION MUSIC SELECTIONS

Receiving Line

Title	Composer	Performed by
_____	_____	_____
_____	_____	_____

Newlyweds' Arrival

_____	_____	_____
_____	_____	_____

Background Music

_____	_____	_____
_____	_____	_____
_____	_____	_____
_____	_____	_____
_____	_____	_____
_____	_____	_____

First Dance

_____	_____	_____

Special Requests (Ethnic, cultural, favorites, etc.)

_____	_____	_____
_____	_____	_____
_____	_____	_____
_____	_____	_____
_____	_____	_____
_____	_____	_____

Cake Cutting Ceremony

_____   _____   _____

Bouquet Toss

_____   _____   _____

Garter Removal

_____   _____   _____

Last Dance

_____   _____   _____

Reception Music and Dancing Selections

Cocktail reception: _____

Receiving Line: _____

Bride/Groom formal introductions: _____

Bride/Groom first dance: _____

Father/daughter dance: _____

Mother/son dance: _____

Cake cutting ceremony: _____

Tossing of Bouquet: _____

Garter Toss: _____

Last Dance: _____

Exit of Bride & Groom: _____

Other: _____

WHAT TO LOOK FOR IN THIS CHAPTER:

- Your wedding photos and video are the lasting memories of your wedding.

- Start early, book early, say "no thank you" to amateurs.

- Have a good rapport with your photo professionals.

- Photo trends in color, black & white, and photojournalism.

- Consider creative wedding album ideas.

- Ask if proofs are included.

- Photographer estimate worksheets.

- "Must have" photo checklist.

- Videographer estimate worksheets.

- "Must have" video scene checklist.

11
PICTURE PERFECT

When all is said and done, your pictures are the lasting memory of your special day. Look for a balanced approach to your wedding photography. I like to offer a mix of portraiture (even if it's casual) and photojournalism. Your wedding video is ultimately for personal use but your wedding photos are shown to everyone.

—Gene Gabelli, Owner
Gabelli Studio, Verona, NJ
www.gabellistudio.com

Recent polls conducted by *theknot.com* asked, "which element are you most willing to go over your budget for?" 26% of the brides answered photography first, reception site was second at 18%, and honeymoon was third at 17%.

Your wedding day is one of the most beautiful days of your life and you will want to capture it on film. Be sure you hire a professional photographer and/or videographer you trust. Nothing is more upsetting than coordinating a beautiful day and then receiving photographs that look amateurish.

HOW TO FIND THE RIGHT PHOTOGRAPHER

- **Start early**. You need to confirm your photographer around the same time as your ceremony and reception sites. Good photographers can be booked up to a year in advance. Be sure to contract the photographer you have chosen, not an assistant or colleague.

> Book your photographer the same time you book your reception site.

- **Ask for referrals**. The best photographers are those who are recommended to you. Ask friends, family, other brides you know, and your caterers for suggestions. Very often florists and photographers work together and know each other, so ask a florist whose work you admire.
- **Interview potential photographers**. Before you make your final decision see at least three candidates and ask to see their work. Ask to see a wedding sample

book, a proof book, and portraitures. Look for consistency in the quality of the photography.

- **Have a good rapport**. Make sure you and the photographer are on the same wavelength. Do you feel confident and relaxed or does he/she make you feel stiff and uncomfortable? If you don't feel relaxed, how do you suppose your family and guests will feel? Does the photographer exude a good attitude toward you and doing your wedding? How experienced is he/she?
- **Consider style**. Many photographers specialize in one or two styles that may not be what you want. Do you want formally posed shots or prefer candids? Do you want all color or a mix of black & white? Can the photographer offer a satisfactory blend of both formal and candid shots for your tastes? The sample books you look at will give an indication of their overall style.

PHOTOGRAPHY TRENDS TO CONSIDER

Consider a variety of modern trends in photography.

Many couples want an album that reflects their taste and something they are proud to display on a coffee table in their home. Gone are the days of a dusty, moldy, wedding album stuck on a bookshelf. Consider these new options.

1. **Black and white photography**. Once the only option for a couple, this style is back in vogue. Be sure your photographer is good with this style and see samples of his/her work. It is important to have proper lighting and shading. Also, tell your makeup artist that your photographs will be black & white—it makes a difference how your makeup is applied.

2. **Photojournalism**. These are cherished natural moments captured by a professional. Rather than posed, stiff shots the photographer roams the site taking candids. Be sure your photographer is experienced in this style. Ask to see his/her work.

CREATIVE WEDDING ALBUMS.

Create a wedding album that you will love in years to come.

ALL CANDIDS—A good photojournalist will cleverly compose a group shot with a relaxed look. If this is a style that appeals to you, your wedding album will have a charming quality of spontaneity.

MAGAZINE STYLE—If you aren't excited by the thought of a traditional album, consider displaying your wedding photos more creatively. One format is the magazine style. Action and reaction shots are fused together to tell a story. Ask the photographer to show you examples of this type of album. Another option is to display photos on an artist-style easel or portfolio with an interesting mat. Ask about including panoramic shots in your selection.

FABRIC ALBUM—Wedding albums covered in fabric are beautiful handcrafted books designed to sit prominently on a table. The designer can create any book cover you want depicting certain elements of your wedding, using fabric. For example, perhaps you have a seaside wedding. The designer selects a fabric and then strategically places motifs on the book. Contact Ann Bruns-Rotunno at *www.bookpenandcandle.com* for creative ideas.

PERSONALIZED CDS—Many photographers now provide a service to display some of your wedding proofs as early as a few days after the wedding. The photographer will design your website and allow you and your guests to view up to 100 photo proofs of the wedding. Request that your photos remain posted on your website for up to sixty days so friends, guests and relatives have ample time to select their favorite photos. They can purchase what they want directly.

CHOOSING A VIDEOGRAPHER

Hiring a photographer and videographer can be a daunting experience. Still shots are a must but a videotape of your wedding can be every bit as necessary. Actions and words gain new life with a good videographer. In both cases you are preserving a moment of your life forever, so you want the best you can afford.

> Hire a professional to videograph your wedding—no amateurs or well-meaning friends.

- **Don't ask an amateur to do the job**. You want someone with state of the art equipment and professionalism. Again, lighting and camera placement are essential. Ask about lighting assistants and other necessary people required for a professional quality tape. Ask about wireless microphones and video carts.
- **Ask for referrals**. Get recommendations and professional advice before you hire a videographer. View several sample tapes. Does the style of the tape coincide with what you want? Ask to see various packages i.e., a one-man camera operation vs. an entire crew. The more people involved the more expensive it is.
- **Consider style**. Do you want a director-type videographer or do you prefer him/her to blend in with the environment? If your personalities don't click look elsewhere.
- **Do you want** simplicity or a grand production?
- **Decide on a package**. Videographers offer different packages at varying costs. The least expensive is a simple one camera, unedited tape provided to you at the end of the reception. The tape includes wedding highlights in order of occurrence. More expensive tapings include a two-man crew, edited version, with an animated beginning, baby picture collage, bride's home, church, reception and flashback ending. The tape is then overlaid with dubbed music and special effects.

THE PHOTOGRAPHER AND VIDEOGRAPHER

All photographers should be professionally trained and attired for your wedding. Be certain that all costs and services are written into contracts. Ask about extras such as lighting, equipment and personnel. Both must be acquainted with your ceremony and reception sites. Firm up dates, times and meeting locations. Make sure your photographer and videographer coordinate camera set-up and lighting placement. Review the quality of their work for clarity, focus, color consistency, and print reproductions.

> Get the "extras" in writing.

Photographers normally provide the bride with an engagement portrait, wedding portrait, wedding proofs, a wedding album and parents' album. Also inquire about CDs and thank-you photo cards.

It's convenient to own your proofs, as a disturbing habit has emerged in wedding guests in recent years. At one wedding a party member insisted on posing for the photographer all evening, resulting in the couple receiving many photos they didn't want. If you own the proofs you will maintain control over those who tend to use wedding photographers to their own ends. You did not intend to pay for their portrait but you'll end up doing so if they can get it from your photographer. Additionally they will be after you for their copies before the champagne has chilled.

Make sure your photographer/videographer can control "camera hogs."

If you see your film being used up on the wrong people put a stop to it, or delegate the responsibility to a trusted guest. After all, film used on incidental guests is film lost on everyone else.

PHOTOGRAPHY ESTIMATE WORKSHEET

(Get estimates from a few photographers.)

Estimate 1

Name of Studio: _____

Address: _____

Phone: _____ Fax: _____ E-mail: _____

Photographer's Name: _____

How many assistants needed: _____

Referred by: _____ Phone: _____

Primary style: _____

Arrival Time: _____ Departure Time: _____

Print Selection	How many	$ per print	Cost
Engagement photo	_____	_____	_____
Wedding Portrait	_____	_____	_____
Wedding Album	_____	_____	_____
Parents' Album	_____	_____	_____
Thank-you photo cards	_____	_____	_____

Website Viewing development (specifics): _____

_____

CD-Rom Wedding Highlights (specifics): _____

_____

Date Proofs Are Ready: _____ Date albums are ready: _____

Other (negative, special effects, panorama shots, etc.): _____

_____

_____

_____

Estimate 2

Name of Studio: _____

Address: _____

Phone: _____ Fax: _____ E-mail: _____

Photographer's Name: _____

How many assistants needed: _____

Referred by: _____ Phone: _____

Primary style: _____

Arrival Time: _____ Departure Time: _____

Print Selection	How many	$ per print	Cost
Engagement photo	_____	_____	_____
Wedding Portrait	_____	_____	_____
Wedding Album	_____	_____	_____
Parents' Album	_____	_____	_____
Thank-you photo cards	_____	_____	_____

Website Viewing development (specifics): _____

_____

CD-Rom Wedding Highlights (specifics): _____

_____

Date Proofs Are Ready: _____ Date albums are ready: _____

Other (negative, special effects, panorama shots, etc.): _____

_____

_____

_____

Estimate 3

Name of Studio: _____

Address: _____

Phone: _____ Fax: _____ E-mail: _____

Photographer's Name: _____

How many assistants needed: _____

Referred by: _____ Phone: _____

Primary style: _____

Arrival Time: _____ Departure Time: _____

Print Selection	**How many**	**$ per print**	**Cost**
Engagement photo	_____	_____	_____
Wedding Portrait	_____	_____	_____
Wedding Album	_____	_____	_____
Parents' Album	_____	_____	_____
Thank-you photo cards	_____	_____	_____

Website Viewing development (specifics): _____

_____

CD-Rom Wedding Highlights (specifics): _____

_____

Date Proofs Are Ready: _____ Date albums are ready: _____

Other (negative, special effects, panorama shots, etc.): _____

_____

_____

_____

&. &. &.

Final choice of photographer: _____

Date Contract Signed: _____

Deposit/Date: _____/_____

Balance Due/Date: _____/_____

Total Cost: _____

"MUST HAVE" PHOTO CHECKLIST FOR PHOTOGRAPHER

Check the photos that you want your photographer capture.

Pre-Ceremony

Bride Getting Ready	**Photo**
• At breakfast	_____
• In hair & makeup	_____
• Finishing dressing, adjusting veil	_____
• Receiving floral bouquets	_____

Bride receiving help from

• Mother	_____
• Father	_____
• Bridesmaids	_____
• Grandparents	_____
• Special relatives	_____
• Bride leaving with escort for ceremony	_____

Groom

• Alone waiting	_____
• With best man	_____
• Father	_____
• Grandparents	_____
• Special relatives	_____
• Groomsmen receiving boutonnieres	_____

At the Ceremony

• Guests Mingling & Arriving	_____
• Ushers escorting guests	_____
• Young attendants distributing programs	_____
• Bride waiting with escort/father	_____
• Parents/step-parents/grandparents being seated	_____
• Bride's mother being seated	_____
• Musicians	_____
• Entire Ceremony (starting with ushers at altar through the exit of bride & groom)	_____

Immediately After Ceremony

• Signing and witnessing marriage certificate	_____
• Guests showering couple with rice, bubbles, petals, etc.	_____
• Couple proceeding to reception (via limo, etc.)	_____
• Other special shots	_____

Pre-determined Shots Before the Reception (Formal Family Photos)

Bride & Groom together with   **Photo**

- Parents (his) _____
- Parents (hers) _____
- Step-parents (his) _____
- Step-parents (hers) _____
- Grandparents (his) _____
- Grandparents (hers) _____
- Bridal party _____
- Child attendants _____
- Officiant _____
- Entire wedding party _____
- Groom with ushers _____
- Bride with ushers _____
- Both families together _____
- Other _____
- Other _____

Reception Favorites

- Room Set-up _____
- Receiving Line _____
- Couple's entrance _____
- Cocktail Reception candids _____
- Receiving toasts _____
- The cake _____
- Cake cutting and sharing _____
- Bridal bouquet toss _____
- Garter toss _____
- Photo of each guest table _____
- Other _____

Dance Favorites

- Couple _____
- Bride & Father _____
- Groom & Mother _____
- Both sets of Parents exchanging dances _____
- Bridesmaids with ushers _____
- Children _____
- Guests _____
- Special ethnic dances _____
- Line dances _____
- Fun scenes _____
- Other _____

VIDEOGRAPHY ESTIMATE WORKSHEET

(Get estimates from a few videographers.)

Estimate 1

Name of Studio: _____

Address: _____

Phone: _____ Fax: _____ E-mail: _____

Photographer's Name: _____

How many assistants needed: _____

Editing Time: _____

Delivery Format: DVD   VHS   Raw footage

Finished Delivery Date: _____

Referred by: _____ Phone: _____

Estimate 2

Name of Studio: _____

Address: _____

Phone: _____ Fax: _____ E-mail: _____

Photographer's Name: _____

How many assistants needed: _____

Editing Time: _____

Delivery Format: DVD   VHS   Raw footage

Finished Delivery Date: _____

Referred by: _____ Phone: _____

Estimate 3

Name of Studio: _____

Address: _____

Phone: _____ Fax: _____ E-mail: _____

Photographer's Name: _____

How many assistants needed: _____

Editing Time: _____

Delivery Format: DVD   VHS   Raw footage

Finished Delivery Date: _____

Referred by: _____ Phone: _____

❧ ❧ ❧

Final Videographer Choice: _____

Date Contract Signed: _____

Deposit/Date: _____ / _____

Balance Due/Date: _____ / _____

Total Cost: _____

Location Scenes

A good wedding video is like a documentary film. When choosing a videographer for your wedding it is important to let the videographer know what "scenes" are important to you, so that you end up with the tape that you want.

Ceremony Rehearsal	_____
Rehearsal Dinner	_____
Bride & Groom getting ready	_____
Pre-ceremony	_____
Full ceremony	_____
Park & formal session	_____
Full Reception	_____

Additional Scenes

Pre and/or post wedding interview	_____
Final dress fitting	_____
Tuxedo pick up	_____
Family thoughts	_____
Other	_____

For video samples go to *www.smileweddings.com* contact Marc Smiler, Video Artist

ADDITIONAL NOTES:

WHAT TO LOOK FOR IN THIS CHAPTER:

- Express your style with flowers.

- Key questions to ask your florist.

- Floral arrangments consist of 3 parts: ceremony, reception and personal bouquets.

- Ceremony flowers: rules to follow.

- Reception flowers: rules to follow.

- Bouquets—bride's bouquet, attendants, boutonnieres, VIP flowers.

- Saving your bouquet.

- Florist estimate worksheets

- Floral checklist—ceremony, reception, bouquets.

12
FABULOUS FLOWERS

The dream bride is one who has done her homework before visiting the florist. She should determine her budget and choose flowers she loves. I love it when brides come in with pictures of arrangements and bouquets they have cut out from magazines. It makes my job easier and she gets what she wants. For optimum beauty and longevity select flowers that are in season.

—Dennis Hatzigeorgakis, Floral Designer
Ariston Florist, NY, NY
www.AristonFlorist.com

Creativity is a key element when you consider your floral arrangements. A current trend is to decorate with hot color displays. Unusual combinations such as orange and pink are fashionable. Red is also acceptable for modern weddings. Traditionally, the bride chose all white combinations ranging from pure white petals to pale creamy tones. Pastels are always acceptable and a traditional favorite.

A lovely way to honor multi-cultural customs is to say it with flowers, seeds or pods depicting foreign folklore. Depending on your degree of dramatic interpretation you can select flower arrangements that will suit the style of your wedding and the style of your gown. Also, the flowers you use to decorate do not necessarily have to coordinate with your bouquet flowers.

Before you choose a florist take a good look at your ceremony and reception sites. If your locations are ornate, fewer arrangements may be needed. If your site is stark then your floral arrangements should be more

> Make sure your flowers complement your ceremony and wedding site.

elaborate. Your caterer will define where arrangements are needed. Often times the caterer can recommend a florist who is accustomed to providing arrangements at your location. Here are some questions to ask a florist you are considering.

1. What flowers are the freshest to use for my wedding season? (In-season flowers stay hardy and are the least expensive.)
2. If you are not familiar with my ceremony and reception site, will you make an on-site visit to determine how many arrangements are needed and where to place them?

3. Will you make up three different styles of arrangements so I can choose my favorite for table centerpieces?
4. What is the cost of the floral arrangements, what time will they be delivered, and by whom?
5. Do you provide other decorative arrangements such as potted palms, screens, aisle runners, Chuppahs, trellises or flower stands if they are needed?

Be sure to request a contract stating and itemizing each floral bouquet and arrangement! See *Fabulous Flowers* worksheets page 153.

CEREMONY FLOWERS

Create a focal point with flowers.

The flower arrangements at your ceremony should frame the bride and groom. If it's in a large cathedral, be sure the arrangements are scaled in proportion to flank you. If your ceremony is in a small room consider two arrangements in smaller proportion on pedestals or stands.

Select flowers that coincide with the style of your wedding. If it's formal, then elaborate flowers are more suitable. If you are having a casual beach wedding consider seashell wreaths.

Tree branches, bushes and greenery can add beauty and drama to standard arrangements. Even cacti in terra cotta pots can create stunning effects in the right environment.

Flowers add a real flair to a ceremony when they are done imaginatively and tastefully. Here is one area where you can bring your personal vision to life!

RECEPTION FLOWERS

Consider room proportions when deciding on flowers.

Keep table arrangements above or below eye level.

Consider your reception space. Is it glass and mirrors? A Victorian mansion? A marquise tent in a backyard? What colors dominate the room or environment? Take your cues from what is fixed in place. Choose floral colors that complement the site.

Don't overload the tables with floral arrangements. Café-style tables look lovely with a tiny bud arrangement or a single floating orchid on a reflective mirror. Large banquet tables need low-level spray arrangements or tall candleabra designs. For a really exotic look ask for tall vases with cascading flowers. Be sure the arrangements are either above or below eye level so your guests can talk.

Consider cultural traditions in lieu of standard arrangements. Stalks of lavender can add a French Provencal touch to a table. Lotus blooms can tie into a Japanese tradition. An island favorite combines coconuts and palms. Research some traditions that coincide with your backgrounds. Do some research to discover what colors are cultural traditions that you can include in your wedding arrangements.

Wherever there is a focal point in the room is where you need flowers. It might be the entrance, the stairs, the mantels, the buffet tables, perhaps the stage where the band performs and/or the ladies room. Ask your florist what is tasteful but not overkill.

If flowers alone are not quite sufficient, ask your florist to create a "light" arrangement with candles, lamps or miniature light strings. This can be especially effective if you use lots of greenery intertwined with light sources. Mirrors also give a reflective quality to candles and lights.

BOUQUET FLOWERS

How about an herb bouquet?
What suits your gown best?

Historically the bridal bouquet was a symbol of fertility. The bouquets were made from special herbs believed to fight evil spirits. Many modern brides are discovering the beauty of herbal bouquets or herbal table arrangements rather than floral bouquets. You may want to try a combination. Decide which style of bouquet works best with your gown and have a silk one made. Later you can toss this one at the reception to one of your lucky bridesmaids.

Do you like the look of a round nosegay or a cascading bouquet? Consider long stem calla lilies tied with ribbons if you are the dramatic type. You may want to carry a treasured bible with flower streamers. Consult your florist for the latest trends and share your ideas with him/her.

To match or not to match?
White, bright or pastel—
you decide.

BRIDESMAIDS BOUQUETS

If traditional symmetry is your desire, then follow the rules of matching bouquets for your bridesmaids. Yours, of course, is the only one that is different and outstanding. Your maid/matron of honor carries a bouquet a bit larger than other bridesmaids. Modern trends ignore symmetry and create different bouquets for each bridesmaid. Look at bridal magazines and the Internet for ideas. Decide how many other women need flowers. Ask your mother and his for suggestions on what type of flowers they want. Wristlets, corsages or purse flowers may be preferred. Don't leave out grandmothers, second wives or special participants. Flower girls usually carry a flower basket.

BOUTONNIERES

During the Middle Ages the groom wore his bride's "colors." This tradition continues today. Many brides select a color from their bouquet and have men's boutonnieres made. The groom's boutonniere is different and slightly larger than the ushers. Roses are the traditional choice but don't rule out carnations, orchids or other flowers. Decide how many other men need boutonnieres including fathers, grandfathers, and other participants.

A BOUQUET TO SAVE

Some brides want to preserve their bouquets as a keepsake. Check first with your florist to determine which flowers are suitable for preservation. Here are some ideas to keep your bridal bouquet "alive."

1. Hang your bouquet upside down in a dark dry place for two weeks. When it is dry decide where you want to display it in your new home. Choose some place where you look but don't touch—dried arrangements are extremely delicate.

Fabulous Flowers

2. Remove the flowers from their stems and place between tissues inside a heavy book. Create pressure by adding more books and leave for two weeks. When they are dry, paste the petals in a frame around a wedding photo or place them in your wedding album.

3. Make a wedding potpourri. Remove each petal from your fresh bouquet and place them in a flat bottom dish so they dry evenly. Don't expose to sun or wind. When they are dry in two weeks, gently place them in a favorite bowl and add your favorite essential oil fragrance.

FABULOUS FLOWERS WORKSHEET

Name of Florist Shop: _____

Address: _____

Phone: _____ Fax: _____ E-mail: _____

Contact: _____

Total Cost: _____

Contract signed: _____ Deposit/date: _____

Balance due/date: _____

Delivery date: _____ Time: _____

DELIVERY LOCATIONS:

Bridal Party

Address: _____

Phone: _____ Contact: _____

Ceremony Site

Address: _____

Phone: _____ Contact: _____

Reception site

Address: _____

Phone: _____ Contact: _____

WEDDING PARTY FLOWERS

BRIDE'S PARTY

Bridal Bouquet:

Choice of flowers (type & color): _____

Bouquet style (cascade, nosegay, etc.): _____

    Ribbon choice: _____ Size: _____

Bride's Tossing Bouquet: _____

    Ribbon choice: _____ Size: _____

Maid/Matron of Honor:

Choice of flowers: _____

Bouquet style: _____

    Ribbon choice: _____ Size: _____ # Needed: _____

Bridesmaids:

Choice of flowers: _____

Bouquet style: _____

    Ribbon choice: _____ Size: _____ # Needed: _____

Flower Girl(s):

Choice of flowers: _____

Bouquet style: _____

    Ribbon choice: _____ Size: _____ # Needed: _____

Mother of Bride:
Choice of flowers: _____
Corsage/wristlet/other: _____ Ribbon choice: _____

Mother of Groom:
Choice of flowers: _____
Corsage/wristlet/other: _____ Ribbon choice: _____

Stepmothers/Grandmothers/Aunts, etc.
Choice of flowers: _____
Corsage/wristlet/other: _____ Ribbon choice: _____ # Needed: ___

GROOM'S PARTY

Groom's Boutonniere:
Flower choice: _____ Color: _____

Groomsmen/Ushers:
Flower choice: _____ Color: _____ # needed: _____

Fathers:
Flower choice: _____ Color: _____ # needed: _____

Stepfathers/Grandfathers/Uncles, etc.: _____
Flower choice: _____ Color: _____ # needed: _____

Ring bearer(s):
Flower choice: _____ Color: _____ # needed: _____

Others (readers, special performers, participants, etc.):
Style: _____ Color: _____ # needed: _____
Style: _____ Color: _____ # needed: _____
Total Cost: _____

CEREMONY FLOWERS

Placement	Arrangement style	Color	# Needed	Cost
Altar, Chuppah, Canopy	_____	_____	_____	____
Aisle Carpet/Runner	_____	_____	_____	____
Pew Arrangements	_____	_____	_____	____
Windows	_____	_____	_____	____
Doors	_____	_____	_____	____
Railings	_____	_____	_____	____
Staircases	_____	_____	_____	____
Candles	_____	_____	_____	____
Candleholders	_____	_____	_____	____

Ceremony Delivery Information
Ceremony site: _____
Address: _____
Phone: _____ Contact: _____ Date: _____ Time: _____

RECEPTION FLOWERS

Placement	Arrangement Style	Color	# Needed	Cost
Receiving Line	_____	_____	_____	_____
Bridal Table	_____	_____	_____	_____
Attendants Tables	_____	_____	_____	_____
Guest Tables	_____	_____	_____	_____
Book signing table	_____	_____	_____	_____
Guest card table	_____	_____	_____	_____
Bandstand	_____	_____	_____	_____
Mantles	_____	_____	_____	_____
Buffet tables	_____	_____	_____	_____
Cocktail Reception tables	_____	_____	_____	_____
Cake Table	_____	_____	_____	_____
Cake	_____	_____	_____	_____
Cake top	_____	_____	_____	_____
Cake knife	_____	_____	_____	_____
Couple's Champagne Glasses	_____	_____	_____	_____
Favor table	_____	_____	_____	_____
Other	_____	_____	_____	_____

Reception Delivery Information

Reception site: _____

Address: _____

Phone: _____ Contact: _____ Date: _____ Time: _____

Total Cost: _____

WHAT TO LOOK FOR IN THIS CHAPTER:

- The ring and the cake are among the oldest wedding traditions—make yours special.

- Tips to ask your baker about cake decorating, fillings and icings.

- Beyond the wedding cake—the shower cake and groom's cake.

- Cake toppers.

- Important questions to ask while taste testing.

- How to save your wedding cake.

- Bakery estimate worksheets.

- Cake flavor, filling, icing, toppers and decorations worksheet.

- Groom's cake favors.

13
WEDDING CAKE WONDERS

It's your wedding so go for it. Choose a cake flavor you really love and don't worry about everyone else. Cakes are as delicious as they are beautiful. Current fashion trends dictate wedding cake styles too. If bridal gowns are simplistic then cakes are generally decorated simply but elegantly. The more elaborate the gown is, the more embellished the cake is. What's most important? The look and the taste.

—Gail Watson, Owner
Gail Watson Custom Cakes, NY, NY
www.gailwatsoncake.com

The wedding cake was an enduring romantic symbol throughout history and remains so today. The Romans sprinkled cake crumbs over the bride's head symbolizing fertility. Today the wedding cake is a favorite focal point at any wedding. Polite guests remain at the wedding reception until the cake is served and everyone is encouraged to eat a bite, as it brings good luck to the bride and groom. In the southern region of the United States many couples choose a traditional wedding reception whereby only wedding cake and champagne are served.

Cakes are an important part of marriage beginning with the bridal shower cake, the groom's cake and finally the wedding cake. The notion of marriage seems incomplete without a wonderful wedding cake.

CREATIVE WEDDING CAKES

> Be prepared to find a baker for your cake—instead of the caterer.

Even if you forego the bridal shower cake and the groom's cake, you will find shopping for your wedding cake quite a delight. Some caterers will bake a cake for you but don't be surprised if you need to find your own baker. The wedding cake, like the wedding gown, is a very personal matter. The traditional tiered cake can be decorated hundreds of ways. You can use different cakes, fillings and icings.

Decide what flavor you prefer and which filling. Talk to your baker about how you want your cake to look. Some brides want a cake that looks like lace while others want edible flowers, still others prefer pearly piping and fat bows. The shape of your cake is also a consideration. Besides the traditional round, consider a square, or novel shapes like a building or heart. The more elaborate the cake the more costly. Wedding cakes can cost anywhere from $3 to $15 per slice so you may want to sample a few bakeries before deciding on one.

THE BRIDAL SHOWER CAKE

There is a strong likelihood that a cake will be served at one of your showers. You are not responsible for this cake but you may want to get the name of the bakery as one of your resources. A bridal shower cake can be charming, lovely, delicious, and a stunning centerpiece.

THE GROOM'S CAKE

The groom's cake makes wonderful take-home favors.

This is a tradition in some areas of the United States, but not all. It can be served at the rehearsal dinner but most commonly it is placed in small boxes so guests can take it home from the wedding reception as a favor.

Flavors can vary so find out what the groom's favorite is. Chocolate is the most popular. Shapes too, vary, and can really be fun: a top hat, a champagne bottle or favorite hobby shape. A lovely way to package the groom's cake is have it made into miniature squares with monogrammed icing, and placed in small boxes. Be creative and ask your baker for other ideas.

Want decorative ideas? Check ***www.gailwatsoncake.com*** for all of your cake needs.

CAKE TOPPERS

Look in vintage and antique stores for unusual wedding cake toppers.

Your wedding cake top can be very personalized. The classic bride and groom atop the cake are no longer your only options. Consider a cultural topper such as a shamrock made from icing. You may also have a vintage topper from a family member or find one in an antique shop. Ask your baker to spin a sugar figurine of interlocking bells.

Fresh flowers or edible flowers cascading from your cake are also beautiful, and often take the place of a topper. A lovely bouquet of ribbons streaming from the cake is also gorgeous, especially if the ribbons are made from icing. If a French touch suits your style find a French baker and ask about a traditional crème-"crokenbush" cake with candles. It is exquisite and very special.

Some couples want to include a sugar sculpture of man's best friend, Spot, sitting on top of the wedding cake. Overall, most brides try to coordinate their flower colors with the wedding cake colors. Don't shy away from color on your cake. It makes a stunning display and looks more modern than the traditional all white cake.

Toppers make good centerpieces as well. One mother of the bride found enough vintage toppers on *Ebay* to decorate each table at the reception.

QUESTIONS TO ASK A CAKE MAKER

1. Do you make your cakes from scratch or do you use mixes? What flavors can I choose from and what kind of fillings do you have?

> Do the taste test for cake, fillings, and icings.

2. Find out which icings they make and sample all kinds. The gourmet tasters will probably prefer the traditional butter cream frosting but a rolled fondant is also tasty. Ask which icing the baker prefers to work with.

3. How do you decorate the cake? Ask to see photos of other wedding cakes they have made. A talented baker will have an album of his/her best work.

4. How large a wedding cake do I need for the number of guests I have? Can you make an additional sheet cake with exact frosting to be served from the kitchen if I need more and want to cut costs?

5. Do you make a groom's cake? How large should it be and what is the cost if it is boxed as take-home favors?

6. Will my chosen cake "hold up" if my wedding is on a hot day?

7. What kind of toppers do you do and will you work with me if I bring one? Do you work with florists if I decide on fresh flowers?

8. How many tiers do I need?

9. What is the cost of the cake? When and where will you deliver the cake? Is delivery an extra cost? What are the payment arrangements?

SAVING THE CAKE

> Enjoy your cake on your first anniversary.

The top tier of the wedding cake was traditionally considered good luck, and saved for the newlyweds to eat on their first anniversary as a blessing. If you want to save your cake ask your baker what kind of cake is recommended for the top tier only. Ask if they can provide you with an airtight container to freeze the cake. Store in the back of your freezer and enjoy on your first anniversary.

WEDDING CAKE WONDERS WORKSHEET

(Get estimates from 3 bakeries before making your final decision.)

BAKERY #1

Name of Bakery: _____

Baker's name: _____

Address: _____

Phone: _____ Fax: _____ E-mail: _____

Date of Delivery: _____ Time: _____

Date Contract Signed: _____

Deposit/Date: _____/_____ Balance Due/Date: _____/_____

Total Cost: $ _____

WEDDING CAKE

Number of Guests Served: _____

Number of Tiers: _____

Shape: _____

Cake Flavor: _____

Filling Flavor: _____

Icing Flavor: _____

Cake Decoration Style: _____

Cake Topper To Be Used: _____

Special Instructions: _____

BAKERY #2

Name of Bakery: _____

Baker's name: _____

Address: _____

Phone: _____ Fax: _____ E-mail: _____

Date of Delivery: _____ Time: _____

Date Contract Signed: _____

Deposit/Date: _____/_____ Balance Due/Date: _____/_____

Total Cost: $ _____

WEDDING CAKE

Number of Guests Served: _____

Number of Tiers: _____

Shape: _____

Cake Flavor: _____

Filling Flavor: _____

Icing Flavor: _____

Cake Decoration Style: _____

Cake Topper To Be Used: _____

Special Instructions: _____

BAKERY #3

Name of Bakery: _____

Baker's name: _____

Address: _____

Phone: _____ Fax: _____ E-mail: _____

Date of Delivery: _____ Time: _____

Date Contract Signed: _____

Deposit/Date: _____ / _____ Balance Due/Date: _____ / _____

Total Cost: $ _____

WEDDING CAKE

Number of Guests Served: _____

Number of Tiers: _____

Shape: _____

Cake Flavor: _____

Filling Flavor: _____

Icing Flavor: _____

Cake Decoration Style: _____

Cake Topper To Be Used: _____

Special Instructions: _____

Final Bakery Choice: _____

Notes: _____

_____

_____

Final Cost: _____

       ঝ   ঝ   ঝ

GROOM'S CAKE

Groom's Cake Desired: yes   no

Cake Flavor: _____

Cake Filling: _____

Cake Icing: _____

Shape: _____ Size: _____ Cost: _____

Boxed As Favors: yes   no

# of Boxed Mini Cakes: _____

Sheet cake: yes   no

Size: _____ # of Servings: _____ Cost: $ _____

Notes: _____

_____

_____

Final Cost: _____

WHAT TO LOOK FOR IN THIS CHAPTER:

- Reasons to wear—or not wear—white

- Explore your gown shopping options.

- Choosing a gown that fits and flatters.

- Choosing a gown that coincides with the style of your wedding.

- Do's and Don'ts for bride and groom's attire.

- Estimate worksheets for bridal gown.

- Worksheet for bridal gown selection and accessories.

- Worksheets for bridesmaids' dresses, accessories, and flowergirls.

- Checklist finale for the bride and her attendants.

14
BRIDAL GOWNS AND WEDDING APPAREL

> *You know you have found the perfect wedding gown when you can imagine loving how you look in your wedding pictures ten years later. Be truthful with yourself. If a little voice is saying to you, "what was I thinking" keep looking for the perfect gown with classic lines that fits and flatters you.*
>
> —Amanda L. Craft, Manager
> David's Bridal, Springfield, PA
> www.davidsbridal.com

Y
ou are the star of the day and all eyes are on you. Your wedding gown is probably the most expensive dress you will buy so it is important to determine which style and silhouette is most flattering to you. Before you make your final decision be sure to try on headpieces and accessories with the gown, to assess a total look.

> Don't despair—Bridal gowns run small.

When you shop for your gown, wear undergarments and shoes that you would wear for a dressy occasion. It's a good idea to take a strapless bra and wear hosiery. Most gowns are American sample sizes eight to twelve and tend to run small, so don't worry if you are normally a size six but fit a size ten. Take your time shopping for a gown and begin at least six months prior to your wedding. It's not uncommon for many brides to shop for their gown a year in advance. Count on at least two fittings to get it just right for your figure.

WHY WEAR WHITE?

The earliest record of brides wearing white was in Egypt. White symbolized virginity and celebration. During World War II, white fabric was the only fabric exempt from U.S. government rationing. Queen Victoria chose white lace, as it symbolized love and romance. Today most brides choose white or ivory, but trendy fashion houses report a surge in sales of pastel shades such as ice blue, mint, lilac and blush. It is interesting to note that during the Middle Ages, brides chose any color they wished as long as it was a superior quality fabric. Many brides who marry more than once prefer a pastel color dress rather than traditional white.

WHERE TO SHOP?

Do your gown shopping with *one* fashion savvy friend.

With Internet access you can view thousands of gowns without leaving your home. *TheKnot.com* or *WeddingChannel.com* are such resources for gowns. Bridal magazines such as *Bride's* and *Modern Bride* also feature hundreds of gowns and offer proper fit and buying tips. Bridal fairs routinely sponsor fashion shows so you can view gowns on models. Check your local newspaper or look in bridal magazines for a schedule of bridal fairs in your area.

After you have done your homework you will want to make the rounds. Begin with the largest bridal salon/department store in your area and make an appointment. They will have the widest assortment of gowns for you to try on and the proper staff to help you. Most brides are surprised to learn that what they thought they wanted is opposite from what they end up buying. Do yourself (and the store) a favor—take only one person with you to be your advisor. Select someone fashion savvy and conscientious about choosing a gown that is in your best interest.

Above all, be sure you love the gown you choose, and that you feel as good as you look in it. Most stores require a 50% deposit when you order. Ask about the store's policy on exchanges, cancellations, refunds, alterations and delivery dates before you sign the bill of sale.

CUSTOM DESIGN GOWNS

Can't find the perfect dress? Consider a custom designed gown. Schedule an appointment with the designer and look at his/her work. Most designers have photos and samples. They'll sketch a basic idea of what looks best on you. Be prepared for multiple fittings beginning with your dress made from muslin.

The advantage to a custom gown is a perfect fit, a gown suited to you, and the exact amount of embellishment (including veil and accessories.) Another advantage is that most designers can complete a gown for you in record time, less than two months, if time is an issue. Designers are experts at camouflage and they are trained in color, silhouette, proportion and bodyline. If you decide to work with a designer, tell them what you like but allow the designer to do his/her job. The extra time is worth the effort and price.

GOWN STYLES

Most brides prefer a traditional wedding gown but fashion trends carry enormous impact whether you realize it or not. Wedding gown trends can change from Victorian modesty to Victoria's Secret sexy in just a few seasons.

Think about how you will look in your wedding photos. If your gown is traditional and simple, chances are you will enjoy your photos in years to come. If you choose a

Select a gown that will stand the test of time in your photos.

trendy look, your photos will not stand the test of time. Don't choose a look that is too casual for the occasion. Even if you decide on a backyard wedding you should celebrate the day with a dress worthy of the occasion.

You can virtually "shop 'til you drop" viewing gowns on websites. Today you can be fashionable, traditional and appropriate if you take the time to browse. Be careful to patronize secure sites with a professional demeanor. Take note of names you recognize from bridal catalogues that you can get from bridal retail stores, or a bridal magazine.

PerfectDetails.com is a high-end site that supplies couture designer accessories to you even if you are in the middle of nowhere. Best of all, they use a highly dependable shipping service. Pay attention to the information any good website offers about it's company, as well as their demeanor when dealing with potential customers. Find out shipping rates and length of time to receive. It doesn't help to order hard to find fashions from a source that cannot deliver on time.

Consider accessories that complement the dress.

But remember, fashions are cyclical. Demure and covered up may, in five years, become strapless and/or backless. Begin by determining your body type before you go shopping so you are better prepared to choose an appropriate gown, then consider if it fits your vision of your wedding. Have fun with style, order Fit & Figure Wheels from *www.curve-style.com*.

WHAT STYLE GOWN FITS YOUR WEDDING?

The more formal the wedding, the more formal the gown… and vice versa. Here is a traditional guideline to help you get the gown and accessories appropriate for you, but remember that it is just a guide. After all, you should be wearing the dress, not letting the dress wear you!

MOST FORMAL

Gowns of pomp and circumstance.

This style is ultra conservative, traditional and elaborate. Think high mass of a grand proportion, ceremony performed in candlelight.

The dress has a cathedral train (extends 6 – 12 feet from waist) with a floor-length gown in white or off white. Wear a floor-length veil, opera-length gloves, matching closed-toe shoes and carry a lavish bouquet plus prayer book. The bodice is covered, as well as the arms. The wedding party is extremely formal and the groom wears tails. Black tie is requested on invitation. Think of Princess Diana's wedding gown or Princess Grace.

VERY FORMAL

Serious gowns without the pomp and circumstance.

Cathedral or chapel-length (extends 3- 5 feet from waist) train with floor length gown. Gown is less elaborate than Most Formal. The veil matches the length of gown. Gloves are optional; shoe is closed-toe.

The overall look is covered-up and conservative. The bouquet is elaborate and prayer book optional. Ceremony can be day or evening, and the wedding party is formal—groomsmen wear conservative tuxedos. Black tie is requested on invitation. Think of Sarah Ferguson's wedding gown when she married Prince Andrew.

Bridal Gowns

FORMAL

The preferred style of many brides.

Floor length gown with chapel-length, sweep (gently "sweeps" the floor) or detachable train. Veil can be floor-length or elbow length. Decide which is the best proportion for your body type.

The overall look is less covered up but not evening-ish. Matching open toe shoe is an option as well as gloves—short or elbow length. Bouquet is less elaborate and a simple prayer book is fine. Bridal party is formal but less conservative in style. Groomsmen wear tuxedos of white or black jackets. Cummerbund and tie may contrast tastefully. Black tie on invitation is recommended but not mandatory. Think of Jacqueline Bouvier's marriage to John F. Kennedy.

SEMIFORMAL

The preferred choice of many second-time brides.

Gown is floor length, mid-calf, or knee-length. Fabric and color can be non-traditional. Experiment with pastels and less elaborate fabrics. A chapel-length train, or fishtail sweep is an option but not necessary. A veil is appropriate so long as it is in correct proportion to the dress. Options to a veil could be flowers in hair, a hat, headband, elegant comb, barrette or clip.

Shoes match and can be open toe, close toe, or a strappy sandal heel. Carry an elegant bouquet and/or floral trimmed prayer book. Bridal party can wear long or short dresses in simple fabric. Groomsmen are appropriate in dark solid color suits. Black tie on invitation is not appropriate. Carolyn Bessette's wedding gown was a perfect choice for her marriage to John F. Kennedy Jr.

INFORMAL

A pristine suit can be perfect for an informal wedding.

Although a short dress is most common, consider a ballet length or long length in fine cotton. A dress suit is also appropriate but a pantsuit is difficult to wear unless you have a flair for the bold and dramatic. Pastel colors are great. You may discover the perfect white dress embellished with colorful embroidery. A veil is not necessary and shoes need not match the dress.

A small bouquet is optional or you may decide to carry a single flower. A corsage or wristlet is also okay. Choose any color you wish, ranging from white to pastels—no black. Tell the same to your attendants, who should wear a simple style and solid color. Groomsmen can wear a dark blazer with trousers, shirt and tie or a solid color suit.

FORMAL ATTIRE DOS & DON'TS
Do's

Do   Pay attention to details—they transform the bride from beautiful to radiant.

Do   Select a gown that coincides with the formality and time of day of your wedding.

Do Work with a reputable and service oriented bridal salon that can guide you through the maze of decisions you need to make.

Do Take the exact lingerie and shoes you will wear with you to your first fitting. If something is not right you have time to make adjustments before the next fitting.

Do Count on at least two to three fittings prior to your wedding day.

Do Ask for an extra piece of fabric of the gown for the purpose of matching shoes, bag, etc.

Do Choose your headpiece at the time you purchase your gown or no later than the first fitting. Be sure you wear the headpiece with the gown during your fittings to determine the length of veil that looks best.

Do Practice walking, sitting and turning in your dress and veil before the big day. You don't want to trip or fall in front of your guests.

Do Practice bustling the train and removing the veil so you know how to detach the fabrics to give you more mobility at your reception. Appoint someone to do this.

Do Have your hair and makeup done professionally. Ask your hairdresser to attach your headpiece and veil for you. Make sure you book a trial date with both.

Do Have lipstick, powder and concealer in your bridal purse for quick touchups.

Do Wear your shoes before your wedding to break them in a bit. Scuff up the soles of the shoes so you don't slip.

Do Have another pair of pantyhose available just in case you get a run—especially if you plan to do the garter routine.

See www.bridalbeauti.com for perfect cosmetics.

DON'TS

Don't Wear evening attire for a daytime wedding.

Don't Ask the groom to wear a tuxedo unless you are having a formal wedding with the reception beginning at 6:00 pm or later.

Don't Have the groom dress exactly like the ushers. He should have details that set him apart from the rest, i.e., formal tails, a contrasting boutonniere, cutaway jacket, etc.

Don't Allow him to wear a pin stripe suit. They're for business.

Don't Ask the groom to wear a tie color or cummerbund that makes him feel too frilly or foolish.

Don't Dress too casually for your wedding even if it is at noontime on the beach. Your appearance helps to honor the occasion, and is a way to celebrate your decision. The same goes for the groom. White shorts on a sailboat may be fine but make sure he wears a jacket and tie.

Don't Ask your bridal party to wear all black or all white. Black is too funereal, and white is appropriate only at a "snowball wedding." You should be the outstanding one—the only one in white at the entire affair.

Don't Leave your attendants, mothers, fathers and important participants in the dark about what you are wearing or planning. Others are guided by what you wear. They need to make decisions about their own dress and they are

Bridal Gowns

waiting for you to set the tone. The mother-of-the-bride chooses first then tells the groom's mother what color and style she is wearing.

Don't Wear a hat unless you are planning an informal outdoor wedding for daytime.

Don't Wear a veil if you are a second time bride as it is considered poor etiquette. The veil is a symbol of virginity and is worn exclusively by a first time bride. Headpieces are fine.

Don't Get a manicure and pedicure the day of your wedding. Do it a day or so in advance so you can dry thoroughly and be calm.

Don't Get a facial or waxing the day of your wedding. Do it at least 7-10 days in advance in case you experience irritations.

Don't Wear red nails or lipstick unless you want a very dramatic contrast.

Don't Get too tan. You will be too difficult to photograph. Be careful of strap marks and tan lines.

Don't Wear makeup that is glittery or shimmer-based. The photos will look harsh, too shiny, and sweaty.

Don't Go all day without eating. You need food to sustain you through the ceremony and reception. You don't want to faint with one glass of champagne. Be sensible—eat.

Don't Expect to eat a full dinner at your reception. Your guests and photographers will keep you very busy.

Most Important: take a break with the groom away from your guests to savor the moment of your wedding. By all means enjoy yourself.

Bridal Gowns

BRIDAL GOWN ESTIMATE WORKSHEETS

Be sure to bring an emergency kit—aspirin, tissues, needle and thread, lipstick, mirror, antacid.

Wedding Dress Estimates

Estimate 1

Name of Bridal Salon: _____Style #: _____ Cost: $ _____

Comments: _____

_____

_____

_____

_____

_____

_____

_____

_____

Estimate 2

Name of Bridal Salon: _____Style #: _____ Cost: $ _____

Comments: _____

_____

_____

_____

_____

_____

_____

_____

_____

Estimate 3

Name of Bridal Salon: _____Style #: _____ Cost: $ _____

Comments: _____

_____

_____

_____

_____

_____

_____

_____

_____

Bridal Gowns

WEDDING DRESS—FINAL SELECTION WORKSHEET

Name of Bridal Salon/Dressmaker: _____ Cost: $ _____

Address: _____

Phone: _____ Fax: _____ E-mail: _____

Store Hours: _____ Contact/Salesperson: _____

Dress Designer: _____ Style #: _____ Size: _____

Dress Fabric: _____ Dress Color: _____

Date Ordered: _____ Delivery Date to Store: _____

Sample Cutting of Fabric Order Date: _____ Receive Date: _____

First Fitting Scheduled: _____

Second Fitting Scheduled: _____

Final Fitting Scheduled: _____

Pick-up Date: _____ Invoice #: _____

Deposit/Date: _____/_____ Balance Due/Date: _____/_____

VEIL/HEADPIECE

Name of store: _____ Cost: $ _____

Address: _____

Phone: _____ Fax: _____ E-mail: _____

Store Hours: _____ Contact/Salesperson: _____

Headpiece Style #: _____ Style of Veil: _____

Date Ordered: _____ Delivery Date to Store: _____

Pick-up Date: _____

Deposit/Date: _____/_____ Balance Due/Date: _____/_____

SHOES

Name of Store: _____ Dye Charge: $ _____ Cost: $ _____

Address: _____

Phone: _____ Fax: _____ E-mail: _____

Store Hours: _____ Contact/Salesperson: _____

Shoe Style #: _____ Size: _____

Date Ordered: _____ Delivery Date to Store: _____

Date of Dye Match: _____ Fabric Swatch Enclosed: yes   no

Pick-up Date: _____

Deposit/Date: _____/_____ Balance Due/Date: _____/_____

BRIDESMAID DRESSES

Copy these pages, cut into thirds and give them to your attendants for easy tracking. For best results, order bridesmaids dresses from the same store to insure dye lot and size.

Maid/Matron of Honor

Name of Maid/Matron of Honor: _____

Name of Store: _____ Cost: $ _____

Address: _____

Phone: _____ Fax: _____ E-mail: _____

Store Hours: _____ Contact/Salesperson: _____

Dress Style #: _____ Color: _____ Size: _____

Date Ordered: _____ Sample Cutting: yes _____ no _____

Delivery Date to Store: _____

Fitting Date: _____ Pick-up Date: _____

Deposit/Date: _____/_____ Balance Due/Date: _____/_____

Bridesmaid

Name of Bridesmaid: _____

Name of Store: _____ Cost: $ _____

Address: _____

Phone: _____ Fax: _____ E-mail: _____

Store Hours: _____ Contact/Salesperson: _____

Dress Style #: _____ Color: _____ Size: _____

Date Ordered: _____ Sample Cutting: yes _____ no _____

Delivery Date to Store: _____

Fitting Date: _____ Pick-up Date: _____

Deposit/Date: _____/_____ Balance Due/Date: _____/_____

❧ ❧ ❧

Name of Bridesmaid: _____

Name of Store: _____ Cost: $ _____

Address: _____

Phone: _____ Fax: _____ E-mail: _____

Store Hours: _____ Contact/Salesperson: _____

Dress Style #: _____ Color: _____ Size: _____

Date Ordered: _____ Sample Cutting: yes _____ no _____

Delivery Date to Store: _____

Fitting Date: _____ Pick-up Date: _____

Deposit/Date: _____/_____ Balance Due/Date: _____/_____

Bridal Gowns

Name of Bridesmaid: _____

Name of Store: _____ Cost: $ _____

Address: _____

Phone: _____ Fax: _____ E-mail: _____

Store Hours: _____ Contact/Salesperson: _____

Dress Style #: _____ Color: _____ Size: _____

Date Ordered: _____ Sample Cutting: yes _____ no _____

Delivery Date to Store: _____

Fitting Date: _____ Pick-up Date: _____

Deposit/Date: _____/_____ Balance Due/Date: _____/_____

ಌ ಌ ಌ

Name of Bridesmaid: _____

Name of Store: _____ Cost: $ _____

Address: _____

Phone: _____ Fax: _____ E-mail: _____

Store Hours: _____ Contact/Salesperson: _____

Dress Style #: _____ Color: _____ Size: _____

Date Ordered: _____ Sample Cutting: yes _____ no _____

Delivery Date to Store: _____

Fitting Date: _____ Pick-up Date: _____

Deposit/Date: _____/_____ Balance Due/Date: _____/_____

ಌ ಌ ಌ

Name of Bridesmaid: _____

Name of Store: _____ Cost: $ _____

Address: _____

Phone: _____ Fax: _____ E-mail: _____

Store Hours: _____ Contact/Salesperson: _____

Dress Style #: _____ Color: _____ Size: _____

Date Ordered: _____ Sample Cutting: yes _____ no _____

Delivery Date to Store: _____

Fitting Date: _____ Pick-up Date: _____

Deposit/Date: _____/_____ Balance Due/Date: _____/_____

ಌ ಌ ಌ

Name of Bridesmaid: _____

Name of Store: _____ Cost: $ _____

Address: _____

Phone: _____ Fax: _____ E-mail: _____

Store Hours: _____ Contact/Salesperson: _____

Dress Style #: _____ Color: _____ Size: _____

Date Ordered: _____ Sample Cutting: yes _____ no _____

Delivery Date to Store: _____

Fitting Date: _____ Pick-up Date: _____

Deposit/Date: _____/_____ Balance Due/Date: _____/_____

Bridal Gowns

Name of Bridesmaid: _____

Name of Store: _____ Cost: $ _____

Address: _____

Phone: _____ Fax: _____ E-mail: _____

Store Hours: _____ Contact/Salesperson: _____

Dress Style #: _____ Color: _____ Size: _____

Date Ordered: _____ Sample Cutting: yes _____ no _____

Delivery Date to Store: _____

Fitting Date: _____ Pick-up Date: _____

Deposit/Date: _____/_____ Balance Due/Date: _____/_____

❧ ❧ ❧

Name of Bridesmaid: _____

Name of Store: _____ Cost: $ _____

Address: _____

Phone: _____ Fax: _____ E-mail: _____

Store Hours: _____ Contact/Salesperson: _____

Dress Style #: _____ Color: _____ Size: _____

Date Ordered: _____ Sample Cutting: yes _____ no _____

Delivery Date to Store: _____

Fitting Date: _____ Pick-up Date: _____

Deposit/Date: _____/_____ Balance Due/Date: _____/_____

❧ ❧ ❧

Name of Bridesmaid: _____

Name of Store: _____ Cost: $ _____

Address: _____

Phone: _____ Fax: _____ E-mail: _____

Store Hours: _____ Contact/Salesperson: _____

Dress Style #: _____ Color: _____ Size: _____

Date Ordered: _____ Sample Cutting: yes _____ no _____

Delivery Date to Store: _____

Fitting Date: _____ Pick-up Date: _____

Deposit/Date: _____/_____ Balance Due/Date: _____/_____

❧ ❧ ❧

Name of Bridesmaid: _____

Name of Store: _____ Cost: $ _____

Address: _____

Phone: _____ Fax: _____ E-mail: _____

Store Hours: _____ Contact/Salesperson: _____

Dress Style #: _____ Color: _____ Size: _____

Date Ordered: _____ Sample Cutting: yes _____ no _____

Delivery Date to Store: _____

Fitting Date: _____ Pick-up Date: _____

Deposit/Date: _____/_____ Balance Due/Date: _____/_____

Bridal Gowns

Name of Bridesmaid: _____

Name of Store: _____ Cost: $ _____

Address: _____

Phone: _____ Fax: _____ E-mail: _____

Store Hours: _____ Contact/Salesperson: _____

Dress Style #: _____ Color: _____ Size: _____

Date Ordered: _____ Sample Cutting: yes _____ no _____

Delivery Date to Store: _____

Fitting Date: _____ Pick-up Date: _____

Deposit/Date: _____/_____ Balance Due/Date: _____/_____

&. &. &.

Name of Bridesmaid: _____

Name of Store: _____ Cost: $ _____

Address: _____

Phone: _____ Fax: _____ E-mail: _____

Store Hours: _____ Contact/Salesperson: _____

Dress Style #: _____ Color: _____ Size: _____

Date Ordered: _____ Sample Cutting: yes _____ no _____

Delivery Date to Store: _____

Fitting Date: _____ Pick-up Date: _____

Deposit/Date: _____/_____ Balance Due/Date: _____/_____

&. &. &.

Flower Girl (s)

Name of Flower Girl (s): _____

Name of Store: _____ Cost: $ _____

Address: _____

Phone: _____ Fax: _____ E-mail: _____

Store Hours: _____ Contact/Salesperson: _____

Dress Style #: _____ Color: _____ Size: _____

Date Ordered: _____ Sample Cutting: yes _____ no _____

Delivery Date to Store: _____

Fitting Date: _____ Pick-up Date: _____

Deposit/Date: _____/_____ Balance Due/Date: _____/_____

Bridal Gowns

ATTENDANTS' ACCESSORIES WORKSHEET

Copy as needed

Shoes for Attendants

Style: _____ Size: _____ Cost $ _____

Fabric swatch included (to match dye lots): yes _____ no ____

Name of Store: _____

Address: _____

Phone: _____ Fax: _____ E-mail: _____

Contact/salesperson: _____

Date ordered: _____ Delivery Date to Store: _____

Dye charge: $ _____ Dye Color #: _____

Pick-up date: _____

Deposit/Date: _____/_____ Balance Due/Date: _____/_____

Hair Ornamentation

Copy as needed

Type of Headpiece (hat, comb, etc.)

  Maid/Matron of Honor: _____

  Bridesmaids: _____

  Flower Girl(s): _____

Name of Store: _____

Address: _____

Phone: _____ Fax: _____ E-mail _____

Contact/salesperson: _____

Maid/Matron headpiece:

  Style #: _____ Color: _____ Quantity: _____ Cost: $ _____

Bridesmaids headpiece:

  Style #: _____ Color: _____ Quantity: _____ Cost: $ _____

Flower girls headpiece:

  Style #: _____ Color: _____ Quantity: _____ Cost: $ _____

Date ordered: _____ Pickup Date: _____

Deposit/Date: _____/_____ Balance Due/Date: _____/_____

Bridal Gowns

BRIDAL ATTIRE CHECKLIST

Gown   _____

Headpiece   _____

Veil   _____

Shoes   _____

Accessories   _____

Hose   _____

Undergarment   _____

Purse   _____

Makeup touch-up kit   _____

BRIDE'S ACCESSORY CHECKLIST

Undergarments

     Bra   _____

     Slip   _____

     Hosiery   _____

     Underwear   _____

     Corset   _____

Accessories

     Necklace   _____

     Earrings   _____

     Gloves   _____

     Purse   _____

     Bracelet   _____

     Garter   _____

     Penny for shoe   _____

     Other   _____

ATTENDANTS CHECKLIST

Undergarments

     Bra   _____

     Slip   _____

     Hosiery (color)   _____

Accessories

     Necklace   _____

     Earrings   _____

     Gloves   _____

     Purse   _____

     Bracelet   _____

     Makeup kit   _____

     Other   _____

Bridal Gowns

ADDITIONAL NOTES/SKETCHES:

Bridal Gowns

WHAT TO LOOK FOR IN THIS CHAPTER:

- Marriage license requirements—can't get married without one.

- Vendor contracts—what to get in writing before you sign.

- Wedding insurance—a good idea for protection.

- Prenuptial agreements—should you have one?

- Wills—protects your wishes in an uncertain world.

- Name change—who needs to know legally and socially?

- Worksheets for marriage license, vendor contracts, wedding insurance, prenuptial agreements, wills and name change.

- Chart of legal age and marriage requirements (Blood test, license applications, expirations, etc.)

15
LEGAL EASE

According to the Bridal Association of America, the average cost of a wedding in the United States is $20,000. In addition to the many service/vendor contracts you will sign, many couples take out wedding insurance. Wedding insurance, pre-nuptial agreements, marriage licenses and wills are a part of marriage in a modern world.

> Keep an open mind and heart towards legal issues.

You and your fiancé should have an open discussion about these sensitive subjects, so you know where you stand. Investigate and really think about these issues well in advance of your wedding day. Forget about the cake and your dress for a moment and concentrate on the legal issues that will protect his and your rights after you are married. Sound cold hearted? A strong relationship withstands honest communication.

MARRIAGE LICENSES

A good way to introduce the discussion of legal matters is with the marriage license. Find out where to apply and when. Find out if you need a blood test. Ask which legal documents to bring with you, i.e. a passport,

> Don't forget to apply for your marriage license.

birth certificate, driver's license. If you are divorced you will need your divorce decree. If you are under the legal marrying age—they vary from state to state—you will need parental consent. If you are widowed you will need your spouse's death certificate.

Finally, ask what form of payment is required for the license fees. Bring cash or money orders, some license bureaus will accept credit cards and checks but don't assume so.

LICENSE CHECKLIST

- Find out where to apply for a marriage license—city/town hall, license bureau, etc.
- Find out when to apply. It's generally two weeks in advance of your date but ask anyway. How long the marriage license is valid for once issued varies by state, and some states have a waiting period once the license is issued prior to allowing a couple to wed.
- If you plan to marry in a foreign country but live in the United States find out what your state's requirements are for a legal marriage. Remember a religious ceremony does not legally bind you—a marriage license does.
- Go together and bring birth certificates (proof of age) and/or passports (proof of residence or citizenship), driver's licenses or form of photo ID, parental consent form (if applicable) and blood test results (if required in your state) .[See chart on page.]
- If you are divorced or widowed, take your divorce decree or the death certificate of the deceased.
- Ask if you need to bring a witness.

Once married, the marriage license will be forwarded to the local marriage license bureau by the officiant. After a few weeks you will receive a certified copy of the marriage license from your state.

BLOOD TESTS

Find out if blood tests are required.

Some states require blood tests, but not all of them. Ask the marriage license office in your locale if they're required, and if so, have your blood work done within a reasonable time prior to the ceremony (two to three months). Don't let your test results expire before you get married. Your primary physician or health care clinic will administer the necessary tests. [See chart on page 185.]

VENDOR CONTRACTS

The following excerpt is a concise plan to review before signing any contracts with service/vendor providers for your wedding.

Planning Your Wedding—Some Legal Considerations by Mikelle V. Lipsius, Esq. of Wagner, Davis & Gold, P.C., New York, ***www.wagnerdavis.com***.

Once you have decided to book a photographer, florist, or any other wedding vendor, it will be necessary to sign a contract with the vendor to formalize the agreement. Here are a few points to consider before signing the contract.

1. Make sure that everything is in writing, including pre-wedding and post-wedding services, materials and finished products that the vendor is to provide. For exam-

ple, when considering a florist, make sure the contract includes the type and approximate size of the flowers the florist is to provide for centerpieces, bridal and attendant bouquets, boutonnieres and any other floral or greenery decorations. Often the contract will include the place where the florist intends to purchase these items, and a backup supplier in the event of a problem.

2. Make sure the contract states which florist will be creating the centerpieces and other decorations you have requested if there is more than one arranger at the flower shop you have selected. (This is very important and also pertains to photographers, videographers and musical entertainment. Don't fall for the bait-and-switch. If you see a vendor's demo tape or sample book and you like what you see, make sure the creator of that demo or book will be the same person performing the services at your wedding. Otherwise the outcome could be disappointing.)

3. The contract should specify the exact number of each item the florist/vendor is to provide and when the items are to be delivered to the ceremony and reception sites.

4. The contract should also state whether the florist/vendor is responsible for placing all or only some of the arrangements or items in their intended places (sometimes the catering facility places floral arrangements on tables once the linens are set).

5. The contract should note who is responsible for removal of flowers, equipment, etc. and when this will be accomplished. Some facilities charge a removal fee for any decorations or equipment left over at the site for longer than twenty-four hours.

Prior to signing the contract, pay careful attention to the liquidated damages clauses of the contract. This provision of the contract explains what will happen if it is necessary to postpone or cancel the wedding. This section usually specifies the sum of money the vendor is entitled to in the event of a cancellation. The sum could be equal or greater than your initial deposit. If the term of the liquidated damages provision seems unreasonable to you attempt to renegotiate putting yourself in a more favorable position in case it is necessary to postpone or cancel the wedding.

The bottom line: don't sign any contract until you read it completely and are satisfied with the terms. If you are concerned with any of the contract provisions, ask the vendor for more time to review the contract. A reputable vendor will have no objections.

WEDDING INSURANCE

Find out the cost and coverage of wedding insurance.

Wedding insurance is a good idea and one you may wish to investigate. An insurance policy will pay in the event of an illness or injury of a severe nature. Wedding insurance can cost in excess of $150 so be sure you understand what is covered and what is not. *The Firemen's Fund* is one company that currently offers wedding insurance coverage.

According to Mikelle Lipsius, Esq. "wedding insurance is designed to protect you and your spouse-to-be in the event of a tragedy, natural disaster, postponement or cancellation of the wedding, personal liability, vendors' services, wedding attire and jewelry, and wedding gifts. As with all insurance a deductible applies as well as a cap on benefits. Check what applies to the policy you have chosen."

Another insurance to look into is your existing homeowners' insurance policy. Although most do not offer wedding insurance you may be able to claim theft or loss of certain items.

By all means, ask what kind of insurance your catering hall has in the event of fire, flood, natural disaster or structural failure. Find out exactly what is and isn't covered before you sign your contract.

NEVER GIVE UP!

In the face of disaster keep your cool and think things through.

Another form of insurance on your wedding day is your own persistence and ingenuity. There is always a chance that things will go awry, but a resourceful couple can save their day.

Inclement weather is always a concern when planning a winter wedding in New England but is rarely an issue for a summer wedding—unless the unexpected happens, as it did to one bride.

A storm of hurricane proportions occurred the day before the wedding. The next day the bride and groom proceeded with their plans in spite of fallen trees, broken power cables and scattered debris. All went well at the church but the reception was a different matter. The entire village lost electricity, including the lovely mansion where the reception was to be held.

The only means of electricity on the premises was a backup generator. The food was cooked on the generator's power but there was not enough electricity for lights or band instruments. As it turned out, the band played acoustically in the mansion lit with candlelight. A potential disaster turned into a romantic, memorable occasion for everyone.

Another bride I know went to her wedding in a milk truck because of a raging blizzard in her town. She had no other means of transportation until she spotted a milk delivery truck gradually making headway. She flagged him and hitched a ride to the church in the nick of time. Fortunately, the bridal party stayed the night before at a hotel within walking distance of the church.

PRENUPTIAL AGREEMENTS

Prenuptial agreements protect your assets and his.

Years ago prenuptial agreements were only relevant to wealthy society. Today they're commonplace. These agreements are difficult to discuss, and even more difficult to implement but they serve a purpose nonetheless.

Prenuptial agreements are geared for the bride or groom who have specific assets they wish to protect in the event that the marriage ends in divorce. As couples establish careers and marry later in life they acquire more assets prior to marriage. It is not uncommon for the bride *and* groom to sign prenuptial agreements particularly if one of the parties is wealthy or has children from a prior marriage. These agreements specify what each person owns and what will happen to these assets in the event of divorce. Ms. Lipsius, Esq. states that "prenuptial agreements define the couples' legal relationship in the event of a divorce. In addition, a prenuptial agreement can be used to protect the holder of an advanced degree such as an MBA, MD or JD, the value of which appreciates over time and is deemed marital property after the wedding. As with all contracts, a prenuptial agreement can only be set aside upon a showing of coercion, duress, fraud or illegality."

Generally there is a time limit to these agreements but it is a good idea to review the documents every few years. Consult your attorney for a review of your agreement and be sure to have both parties sign it, date it, have it witnessed and notarized.

In either case discuss prenuptial issues several months prior to your wedding so you clear the air of any unpleasant thoughts. One couple didn't heed that warning, and as a result suffered through their last week before their marriage.

They were an established older groom and younger bride. She came from a modest background and had few assets. The groom was a prominent business owner.

He had dallied with the idea of a prenuptial but didn't get serious about it until a week prior to the wedding. Instead of tending to last minute wedding details the couple found themselves in separate law offices negotiating issues that could have been dealt with months before.

The language of the terms was harsh, and the negotiations caused tremendous friction. The time spent reaching an agreement was exhaustive, and resentment underscored their wedding day. Not only was the day jaded, the couple suffered totally unnecessary anxiety.

WILLS

A will is another legal issue that is better discussed before marriage. Again, the more established you and your groom are, the more important it is to come to an agreement about what's yours, what's his and how your assets are dispersed in the event of death.

> No one can foresee the future. Make a will—even if you scribble it and fax it to your lawyer. Be sure to sign it.

Granted these discussions are difficult but it's better to put pen to paper and draw up a will that expresses both your wishes than to let things slide. A will is a legal document designed to carry forth your desires at the time of death. We all know stories of couples living without wills and untimely deaths. Their sudden demise can send emotionally vulnerable families spiraling into combat. Life is full of surprises. A will allows the legal system to carry out your wishes as intended. On the subject of wills, Ms. Lipsius, Esq. further states that "wills formalize your intentions especially if there are items you wish to bequeath and devise to those other than your husband. Otherwise, should you pass away in testate, or without a will, all your assets will be distributed according to law, rather than according to your wishes."

Though it may seem insensitive, or in fact macabre, to make decisions such as these before your wedding celebration, it is really the best time to do so. A frank discussion with your fiancé will define your priorities. You can then begin your new life together with total knowledge of your plans for the future. These issues address one of the most intimate sides of married life, and there is no time like the present to clear the air.

It is a statement of fact that more people are willing to discuss their sexual affairs than their financial affairs. So don't be embarrassed about wanting a will.

NAME CHANGE

One more legal issue to decide is whether or not you wish to change your maiden name. If so, you must advise others of the change. Do you want to take your husband's name or hyphenate your last name? Once you have a certified copy of your marriage license the process is relatively simple. Here is a checklist of the various organizations you will need to inform.

- Department of Motor Vehicles—a personal visit will be necessary to update your license so take your marriage license. A new photo and signature will be required.
- Social Security Administration—phone number is 800-772-1213 to implement a name change.
- Insurance companies—contact your auto, health and life insurance providers
- Financial institutions—banks, mortgage holders, credit cards, etc.
- Local post office.
- Voter registration office.
- Utility companies.

In addition you will want to inform your friends, family and social circles of your name change decision. Finally, the business community in which you practice needs to know how you wish to be addressed.

MARRIAGE LICENSE REQUIREMENTS

Marriage license requirements provided by William E. Mariano & Assoc., White Plains, New York. Revised information collected in the year 2002.

State	Common Law Marriage	Minimum Age w/ parental consent	Minimum Age w/o parental consent	Max. period between Medical exam & license	Scope of Medical Exam	Waiting Period before license	Duration of license validity	Wait after license
AL	Yes	14	18	N/R		None	30 days	None
AK	No	16	18	N/R		3 Days	3 months	None
AZ	No	16	18	N/R		None	None	None
AR	No	m-17, f-16	18	N/R		None	None	None
CA	No	none	18	30 days		None	90 days	None
CO	Yes	16	18	N/R		None	30 days	None
CT	No	16	18	N/R	VD	4 Days	65 days	None
DE	No	m-18, f-16	18	N/R		24 Hours	30 days	None
FL	No	16	18	N/R		3 Days	60 days	None
GA	No	16	18	N/R	VD	3 Days	30 days	None
HI	No	15	18	N/R		None	60 days	None
ID	No	16	18	N/R	VD	None	None	None
IL	No	16	18	N/R	VD	1 Day	60 days	1 day
IN	No	17	18	N/R		None	60 days	None
IA	Yes	16	18	N/R		3 Days	30 days	None
KS	Yes	m-14, f-12	18	N/R		3 Days	6 months	None
KY	No	18	18	N/R		None	30 days	None
LA	No	18	18	10 days		None	None	72 hours
ME	No	16	18	N/R		3 Days	90 days	None
MD	No	16	18	N/R		48 Hours	6 months	None
MA	No	m-14, f-12	18	3-60 days		30 Days	60 days	None
MI	No	16	18	N/R		3 Days	33 days	None
MN	No	16	18	N/R		5 Days	6 months	None
MS	No	none	m-17, f-15	30 days	VD	3 Days	None	None
MO	No	15	18	N/R		3 Days	30 days	None
MT	Yes	16	18	N/R	VD	None	180 days	3 days
NE	No	17	18	N/R	VD	2 Days	1 year	None
NV	No	16	18	N/R		None	1 year	None
NH	No	m-14, f-13	18	N/R		3 Days	90 days	None

Legal Ease

State	Common Law Marriage	Minimum Age w/ parental consent	Minimum Age w/o parental consent	Max. period between Medical exam & license	Scope of Medical Exam	Waiting Period before license	Duration of license validity	Wait after license
NJ	No	16	18	N/R		72 Hours	30 days	None
NM	No	16	18	30 days	VD	None	None	None
NY	No	16	18	N/R		None	60 days	24 hours
NC	No	16	18	N/R		None	None	None
ND	No	16	18	N/R		None	60 days	None
OH	No	m-18, f-16	18	N/R		5 Days	60 days	None
OK	Yes	16	18	30 days	VD	None	30 days	None
OR	No	17	18	N/R		3 Days	60 days	None
PA	Yes	16	18	30 days	VD	3 Days	60 days	None
RI	Yes	m-18, f-16	18	N/R	VD	None	3 months	None
SC	Yes	m-16, f-14	18	N/R		24 Hours	None	None
SD	No	16	18	N/R		None	20 days	None
TN	No	16	18	N/R		3 Days	30 days	None
TX	Yes	14	18	N/R		72 Hours	30 days	None
UT	Yes	14	18	N/R		None	30 days	None
VT	No	16	18	30 days	VD	24 Hours	None	3 days
VA	No	16	18	N/R		None	60 days	None
WA	No	17	18	N/R		3 Days	60 days	None
WV	No	18	18	N/R	VD	3 Days	None	None
WI	No	16	18	N/R		5 Days	30 days	None
WY	No	16	18	N/R	VD	None	None	None
DC	Yes	16	18	30 days	VD	3 Days	None	None
PR	No	m-18, f-16	21	N/R	VD	None	None	None

LEGAL EASE WORKSHEET

Marriage License & Blood Test

Is a blood test required in your state?   yes _____   no _____

Date of Test: _____ Expiration Date: _____

Where to apply for a marriage license (couple must appear together)?

_____

Address: _____

Phone: _____ Hours: _____

When to Apply (number of weeks prior to wedding): _____

Checklist of legal documents you need to take:

Blood test _____ Birth certificate _____

Passport _____ Photo ID/drivers license _____

Divorce Decree _____ Death Certificate _____

Parental Consent _____

Marriage license fee $_____

Form of Payment: _____ cash _____ money order _____ credit card _____ check

Vendor Service Contract Checklist

The following vendors will provide you with a contract or letter of agreement. Make sure you have written agreements with these service providers.

- Bakery
- Bridal Consultant
- Bridal dress shop
- Caterer
- Ceremony site
- Florist
- Men's formalwear store
- Musicians
- Officiant
- Photographer
- Rental companies (tents, tables, etc.)
- Rental hall
- Transportation companies
- Videographer

1. **Put it in writing.** List all pre and post wedding services to be provided. Be specific about details, costs, deposits and delivery dates. Include backup suppliers when necessary.

2. **List names of specific individuals who will be providing a service.** For example, if you hire a certain musician or photographer make sure you include his/her name on the contract.

3. **Include the exact number of items plus date and time of delivery.** For example specify how many floral arrangements are needed and where each is to be delivered.

4. **Specify who is to place or set up items you have ordered.** Who will arrange chairs? Who will be responsible for centerpieces?

5. **Agree on who is responsible for equipment removal.** If flowers are left who will remove them? What are the stipulations for returning rented tents, tables, chairs or tuxedos?

Legal Ease

6. **Pay attention to the liquidated damages clauses of contracts.** In case it is necessary to postpone or cancel the wedding, be aware of cancellation fees and be prepared to renegotiate.

7. **Read it thoroughly.** Sign contracts only when you are sure you understand its contents completely. Know what you are getting, when you get it, where you will get it from, who will be providing the service, and what the costs are. Spell out the deposits for down payments, overtime charges, gratuities and final balance due dates.

8. **Sign and date the contract and have the vendor do the same.** A contract is only valid when signed by both parties.

Wedding Insurance

Name of Insurance Company: _____

Contact: _____

Phone: _____ Fax: _____ E-mail: _____

Policy Number: _____ Coverage: _____

Deductible: $ _____

Total cost: $ _____

Prenuptial Agreements

Prenuptial agreements define the couple's legal relationship in the event of a divorce. Use this space to list assets you wish to protect. You may wish to include advanced degrees such as M.B.A., M.D., Ph.D., etc.

Bride's Assets   Groom's Assets

_____   _____

_____   _____

_____   _____

_____   _____

_____   _____

_____   _____

_____   _____

_____   _____

Wills

Though a will is a low priority for an excited bride, having one will ease your mind and those of your loved ones in an uncertain world. If you wish to bequeath some of your assets to someone(s) other than your husband having a will allows you to do so. Consider the following:

Assets (stocks, bonds, property): _____

_____

_____

_____

Real Estate: _____

_____

_____

Heirloom(s): _____

_____

_____

Jewelry: _____

_____

_____

Name Change

If you decide to change your name you need to inform legal organizations as well as your family and friends. Here is a checklist.

____ Department of Motor Vehicles

____ Social Security Administration – phone 800-722-1213

____ Insurance Companies

____ Financial Institutions

____ Post Office

____ Voter Registration

____ Utility Companies

WHAT TO LOOK FOR IN THIS CHAPTER:

- The rehearsal party is traditionally the groom's responsibility.

- What the groom will need to know from you.

- Checklist of what you will want him to know.

- No matter how formal, keep the party warm and friendly.

- Who to invite to the rehearsal and party.

- Rehearsal Party guest list worksheets.

16
THE REHEARSAL PARTY

> *Here's to the husband*
> *And here's to the wife*
> *May they remain lovers for life.*
>
> —*Toasts* by Paul Dickson

Since this is the groom's responsibility, you can sit back and enjoy this party to the fullest. Make it a point to delegate this responsibility early on so you don't waste time and energy worrying about it, especially if he needs to book a restaurant in advance. Let him bounce ideas off of you but don't be drawn into it to the point where it ends up your responsibility. Truly, the best part of the rehearsal dinner is that it's your chance to relax and enjoy before the big day—so let yourself!

Be sure to introduce out-of-towners to your friends and family.

THINGS TO REMEMBER WHEN PLANNING THE REHEARSAL PARTY HE CAN'T LIVE WITHOUT....

- It's your turn to relax.
- Traditionally, the rehearsal party was the groom's responsibility to host.
- Date, time, location, phone number and directions to your rehearsal and rehearsal party.
- Party guest list and phone numbers.
- Additional guest list, like reader, officiant, out-of-town close friends/family; and phone numbers.
- Food and beverage costs.
- Entertainment costs.
- Flowers and decoration costs.
- Tips, transportation and miscellaneous costs.
- Dessert or groom's cake.

By the time of the rehearsal party, you are all pretty familiar with your new families. Like your engagement party, be on time and attentive to your guests. Be sure to introduce out-of-town guests that may have been absent until this night.

A toast by anyone who would like to speak is a nice idea now because everyone is becoming excited about your big day. Any good sentiments will warm hearts all the way around.

Rehearsal dinners/parties can be as lavish as the wedding or casual as a backyard barbecue. Plan your party within a reasonable distance from the ceremony site. If distance becomes a factor then gauge your time accordingly. Do you have a complete guest list of who you are inviting to the rehearsal and dinner? It is a nice gesture to invite your officiant to your rehearsal party even if you do not know him/her very well.

Be sure to make the rounds after your meal, and say your goodbyes to all before the night goes too late. Others may enjoy a few drinks but tonight is your time to say one last goodbye as single people and go home to unwind. The best and only preparation you can make at this point is to sleep well and wake up refreshed.

Don't forget to thank everyone that made your day possible, and especially to stand back and take in your last evening as a single woman.

THE REHEARSAL PARTY WORKSHEET

The Guest List—*copy as needed*

Traditionally the groom pays for this party. You may decide to invite other special people in addition to the wedding party. Start with all bridesmaids and their dates/spouses, all groomsmen and their dates/spouses. Invite both sets of parents and stepparents; include child attendants and their parents. If budget allows widen the circle of invitations to include grandparents, clergy(s)and soloists. Out-of-towners are especially honored to be invited.

Name: _____

Address: _____

Phone: _____ Fax: _____ E-mail: _____

Attendance: Yes   No

Name: _____

Address: _____

Phone: _____ Fax: _____ E-mail: _____

Attendance: Yes   No

Name: _____

Address: _____

Phone: _____ Fax: _____ E-mail: _____

Attendance: Yes   No

Name: _____

Address: _____

Phone: _____ Fax: _____ E-mail: _____

Attendance: Yes   No

Name: _____

Address: _____

Phone: _____ Fax: _____ E-mail: _____

Attendance: Yes   No

Name: _____

Address: _____

Phone: _____ Fax: _____ E-mail: _____

Attendance: Yes   No

THE REHEARSAL PARTY GUEST LIST

Name: _____

Address: _____

Phone: _____ Fax: _____ E-mail: _____

Attendance: Yes   No

Name: _____

Address: _____

Phone: _____ Fax: _____ E-mail: _____

Attendance: Yes   No

Name: _____

Address: _____

Phone: _____ Fax: _____ E-mail: _____

Attendance: Yes   No

Name: _____

Address: _____

Phone: _____ Fax: _____ E-mail: _____

Attendance: Yes   No

Name: _____

Address: _____

Phone: _____ Fax: _____ E-mail: _____

Attendance: Yes   No

Name: _____

Address: _____

Phone: _____ Fax: _____ E-mail: _____

Attendance: Yes   No

Name: _____

Address: _____

Phone: _____ Fax: _____ E-mail: _____

Attendance: Yes   No

Name: _____

Address: _____

Phone: _____ Fax: _____ E-mail: _____

Attendance: Yes   No

THE REHEARSAL PARTY

Name: _____

Address: _____

Phone: _____ Fax: _____ E-mail: _____

Attendance: Yes   No

            ‌ε⦚ ε⦚ ε⦚

Name: _____

Address: _____

Phone: _____ Fax: _____ E-mail: _____

Attendance: Yes   No

            ε⦚ ε⦚ ε⦚

Name: _____

Address: _____

Phone: _____ Fax: _____ E-mail: _____

Attendance: Yes   No

            ε⦚ ε⦚ ε⦚

Name: _____

Address: _____

Phone: _____ Fax: _____ E-mail: _____

Attendance: Yes   No

            ε⦚ ε⦚ ε⦚

Name: _____

Address: _____

Phone: _____ Fax: _____ E-mail: _____

Attendance: Yes   No

            ε⦚ ε⦚ ε⦚

Name: _____

Address: _____

Phone: _____ Fax: _____ E-mail: _____

Attendance: Yes   No

            ε⦚ ε⦚ ε⦚

Name: _____

Address: _____

Phone: _____ Fax: _____ E-mail: _____

Attendance: Yes   No

            ε⦚ ε⦚ ε⦚

TOTAL GUEST COUNT: _____

WHAT TO LOOK FOR IN THIS CHAPTER:

- Write down a schedule—stick to it.

- Bridal do's—getting ready and being beautiful.

- Bridal don'ts—don't invite trouble.

- Countdown to the ceremony.

- Arriving at the ceremony.

- Breathe, stay focused, stay centered.

- Today's checklist.

- Wedding day agenda worksheet.

17
THE COUNTDOWN
YOUR WEDDING DAY AGENDA

The day is perfect and so are you. Wake-up refreshed and take time to envelop yourself in a silky, warm, aromatherapy bubble bath. Think about the precious day ahead of you and the treasured loved ones that will share it with you. Release all your tensions and allow a smile to appear on your face that will have you glowing all day.

—Susie Galvez, Owner
Faceworks Day Spa, Richmond, VA
www.faceworks@msn.com

The day is finally here. Your planning is done, your guests are arriving, you have completed your rehearsal and now face one of the most special days of your life. The sign of a well-planned wedding is the manner in which the bride handles little details that come up on her wedding day. And, as any bride can tell you, little things will pop up. If you really want to relax you might consider hiring a bridal consultant for the day. (see Chapter 18)

Another essential, which, incidentally, will make you feel more in control, is to make out a schedule for that day. Go from breakfast to beauty appointments to arrival times for your photographer, florist, and any family members. Include times that men arrive at church, in case you need someone to contact them. Having a schedule will help you remember details that seem overwhelming when they're floating around in your head. Put them down on paper, give copies to your fiancé and other key participants, and then let it go so you can focus and relax.

> Write down a schedule of events leading up to the ceremony.
> Attention to little details make giant differences.

BEAUTY AND THE BRIDE: DOS & DON'TS

> Before you panic take 3 deep breaths.

DO   Get a good night's rest the night before.
DO   Wake up early to give yourself plenty of time to get ready.
DO   Have your hair and makeup done professionally (preferably at your place).
DO   Have something to eat prior to the ceremony because you may not eat again today.

DO Hang up your gown and veil. Place shoes, jewelry, gloves, headpiece, hosiery, garter, handbag and bridal undergarments in a specific spot.

DO Give your wedding rings to the best man and/or honor maid to hold at the altar.

DO Last minute packing for your honeymoon.

DO Prepare going away outfit if you are changing from your gown as you leave the reception.

DO Take time to reflect on this glorious day (a quick nap, meditation, or quiet time, alone).

🐛 🐛 🐛

DON'T Stay out partying the night before.

DON'T Decide to make any drastic changes in your appearance the day of your wedding, i.e., hairstyle, hair color or cut. Make these decisions three months prior.

DON'T Decide to have a facial, manicure or pedicure (you won't sit still or relax)

DON'T Answer the phone or make too many unnecessary phone calls. Let someone else speak to your friends, who may mean well but will create extra tension.

DON'T Decide to try a new fragrance or beauty product (now is not the time for possible skin irritations).

DON'T Lose track of time. Ask someone to keep time for you and keep you on schedule, as you won't be wearing a watch, as you get dressed in your wedding gown.

DON'T *PANIC!* The biggest mistakes can be solved if you have given yourself extra time.

COUNTDOWN TO THE CEREMONY

From the moment you leave the hairdresser to the moment you put that dress over your head—carefully—the clock will be ticking. Once the dress is on and makeup done, it won't be possible to move around very much. If you have pre-wedding photos planned, the photographer will arrive an hour prior to your departure, as will bouquets and corsages. If you don't have a plan, you will be pulled in many directions and find yourself on the way to your ceremony before you know it. The following is a rough outline. Tailor it to your own plans.

> Time yourself and stay on track. If others are getting you hyper-kick them out. Spend 15 minutes-alone to reflect and get centered.

As soon as your hair and makeup are done, put on your dress. If you have helpers, be sure they are doing exactly that. If they are confusing you as to what looks good or distracting those who are trying to fix your hair, makeup or dress, kick them out. You only have one shot at this and it is no time for unwelcome opinions and hyper chatter.

One hairdresser I know recommends brides come alone because party members distract attention from the stylist. Some try to take suggestions for their own look from the bride's hair and makeup. This is the day when you should have no qualms about standing out from the crowd—not the day to look like all of your girls. If you followed the advice in Chapter 3 on choosing your maids, this shouldn't be a problem, but if anyone is getting in your way, they should not be present.

After you're dressed, touch up hair and makeup. Then spend 15 to 20 minutes alone so you can really see yourself. This serves dual purposes. You can be sure your appearance is up to *your* standards, no one else's, and you can spend your last precious moments reflecting on this rare day. Take the time to admire how beautiful you look.

TWO HOURS BEFORE

If you are having formal photos taken, arrange with the photographer what time he/she will arrive. Ask the photographer to take all other group shots first and include you at the very end of the photo session for final shots. If you are too nervous to sit for photos, have a couple taken and then send him/her to the church to take the men. Be sure the photographer and videographer have sufficient time to get to the ceremony site to set up the equipment.

> Schedule what time the photographer arrives.

ONE HOUR BEFORE

Coordinate ahead of time with your bridal consultant, maid of honor or person in charge to review the line-up with the bridal party as designated during the rehearsal session. Be sure you have your bouquet and see to it that the "charge person" takes care of distributing all other flowers, corsages, boutonnieres, etc. Remind ushers to fix pew ribbons, distribute prayer books and wedding programs. Ask the best man to double check he has the rings and the marriage license. Also, request that he makes sure the groom is suited properly and well groomed with tie straight, boutonniere in correct position and hair combed (brush away any flaky dandruff or stray hairs).

> Coordinate your final review list with your maid of honor or bridal consultant.

THIRTY MINUTES TO AN HOUR BEFORE

You and your father (or escort) are the last to arrive at the ceremony. Your mode of transportation is pre-set. If your bridal party is being transported via bus, trolley or limousine, etc. let them leave 30 minutes before you. Ushers should be on site at least 45 minutes sooner.

> Spend your last few minutes with your father or escort out-of-site.

Be sure to smooth out the back of your dress before you sit down (you may want to sit on a clean sheet.) Fabrics wrinkle easily and your dress will crush. Be sure to enjoy the scenery as you ride to the ceremony site, it will help you remain calm and stable to take in everything around you as you ride.

Remain with your father or escort until all guests are seated and the bridal party is assembled at the ceremony site. Stay out of view of guests so you don't spoil your entrance. In Christian ceremonies it is considered bad luck for the bride to see the groom prior to her entrance down the aisle.

YOU ARRIVE—THE RADIANT BRIDE

This is it. All of your planning and dreaming is here. Now your wedding begins. Right before you start down the aisle, take some deep breaths to help shake the tension and center yourself. After you've done that, take the most important advice I can give you: Stay in the moment and be present to this extraordinary day.

Breathe, stay focused, and feel the moment.

Your Wedding
Day Agenda

THE COUNTDOWN: YOUR WEDDING DAY WORKSHEET

WEDDING DAY CHECKLIST

_____	Breakfast
_____	Hair stylist
_____	Makeup appointment
_____	Prepare gown, veil, accessories
_____	Complete honeymoon packing
_____	Prepare going away outfit
_____	Confirm photographer/videographer arrival time
_____	Review list with bridal consultant and maid of honor
_____	Bridal line-up, pew ribbons, prayer books, programs, marriage license, rings
_____	Appoint someone to help distribute bouquets, corsages, boutonnieres

WEDDING DAY AGENDA

6:00 AM _____

_____

7:00 AM _____

_____

8:00 AM _____

_____

9:00 AM _____

_____

10:00 AM _____

_____

11:00 AM _____

_____

12:00 AM _____

_____

1:00 PM _____

_____

2:00 PM _____

_____

3:00 PM _____

_____

4:00 PM _____

_____

Your Wedding Day Agenda

5:00 PM _____
          _____

6:00 PM _____
          _____

7:00 PM _____
          _____

8:00 PM _____
          _____

Your Wedding Day Agenda

LAST MINUTE NOTES:

Your Wedding Day Agenda

WHAT TO LOOK FOR IN THIS CHAPTER:

- How to find a bridal/wedding consultant.

- What to expect from a consultant.

- What to ask a consultant.

- How to know when you need a consultant.

- Worksheets to help you coordinate with your consultant.

HIRING A WEDDING CONSULTANT

> *I am asked constantly, why hire a wedding consultant? The answer is simple. I can save you time and money because of the relationships I have developed that service the wedding industry. I can negotiate everything for the best price and at times, I even negotiate between families.*
>
> —Jillian Gurak, Owner
> Wedding Vows Inc., NY, NY
> www.weddingvowsinc.com

Some brides consider the bridal wedding consultant the "angel wings" of the wedding. A good consultant can plan a wedding from start to finish for the bride who is too busy, too disorganized, or totally clueless. They can charge by the hour, the day, or the event.

> When in doubt, hire a professional wedding consultant.

Bridal consultants can work miracles in places where the average couple feel helpless. The cost of a good wedding consultant can be either a flat fee, an hourly rate or a percentage of the total event. Consider how much time you have to plan your wedding and take into consideration where it will be. If it is a long distance wedding and you don't have a contact there to help (the totally clueless bride), a bridal consultant is a must.

Don't worry that you will have no input; he/she will give you recommendations and allow you the final decisions. With the Internet, you can plan a great wedding without touching foot on the continent until your wedding day. To find a wedding consultant in your area (or wedding site) go to *www.bridalassn.com.*

WHAT TO EXPECT FROM A BRIDAL CONSULTANT

Consider hiring a wedding consultant specifically for your wedding day. You do all the pre-planning and the consultant arrives to direct the final event. You can relax while he/she does all the last minute duties and orchestrates the ceremony behind the scene. He/she will also handle reception chores, keep everything on time and on track with the caterer, music professionals, photographer(s), florists, transportation officials, etc. You can also ask the consultant to take care of all tipping and final checks so you are unencumbered.

> A consultant can be hired for the event, the day or per hour.
>
> Consultants can be your most trusted problem solver.

BRIDAL CONSULTANT TO THE RESCUE!

If you encounter a personality problem somewhere along the way (and count on it) a consultant can work wonders. Share the problem and he/she will go about solving it in a professional manner. Just speak up and let the consultant know what is bothering you. One young bride I worked with took particular joy in planning every aspect of her spectacular wedding for more than a year. Everything was perfect and grand. She was married in a prominent Catholic Church in New York City with a formal High Mass during a candlelight ceremony. The reception took place in two grand ballrooms in a palace-like private club.

The bride and groom invited more than 300 guests. Cocktails were served in one ballroom and a formal sit down dinner was served in the other. No expense was spared.

This wedding was the dream of the bride's life—until the best man invited a glamorous Hollywood star to be his date. Suddenly, the bride felt eclipsed, (with good reason) knowing this stunning actress would be at her wedding. Convinced that all eyes would be on the best man's superstar date and she would end up ignored, she became furious and expressed her dismay to her fiancé. The groom felt he couldn't tell his best man who to bring, or not bring, as his date.

An explosion seemed imminent, until the bride mentioned her predicament to her wedding consultant. The consultant explained that the Hollywood star was so famous that either she wouldn't come at all or would make an appearance and not stay the entire wedding. She was right. The star accompanied the best man to the wedding ceremony but was nowhere in sight at the cocktail reception or dinner. Needless to say the bride was off the hook and the star cameo was merely a small point of interest in a gala event.

ETIQUETTE AWARENESS

Although the bride rectified the situation, it should be noted that the best man did not show much etiquette. He should have considered the feelings of the bride, asking her permission before inviting his famous date or perhaps reassuring her that it would be a limited appearance. He looked like a show-off, while she handled the situation with grace.

Unplanned challenges such as the one just described tend to pop up in any event as large as a wedding. It is an emotional day that incorporates many disparate personalities—all emotionally invested in your personal moments. Because of this, it is advisable to plan the things that can be predicted so that unexpected problems can be resolved and forgotten in light of the bigger picture, which should move constantly ahead according to plan.

Know what order the DJ or band will introduce ceremonies, special dances, etc. Work it out with them ahead of time. The same goes for the meal service, photographs, and any other service that will require your attention during the party if you haven't given them direction beforehand. Your reception goes by so quickly, if you forget ceremonies you had your heart set on or make rash decisions, the night will be over before you know it and the opportunity will be missed.

Now is the time to do your homework so you can enjoy your wedding. Your guests will appreciate a smooth, well-planned party and you will have what you want: a beautiful day. Isn't that what it's all about? Don't direct your own wedding. Hire a consultant.

THE WEDDING CONSULTANT WORKSHEET

A Wedding Consultant helps coordinate the wedding day events. A bridal consultant coordinates the bride's personal agenda. Some consultants do both.

Name of Consultant: _____

Address: _____

Phone: _____ Fax: _____ E-mail: _____

Services Needed: _____

_____

_____

_____

_____

_____

_____

_____

Additional Services Needed: _____

_____

_____

_____

_____

_____

_____

_____

_____

_____

Fee Structure

    Percentage of wedding: _____

    Per Diem: _____

    Per hour: _____

    Flat fee: _____

Contract Signed/Date: _____/_____

Deposit/Date: _____/_____

Balance Due/Date: _____/_____

19

*B*RIDAL *G*OWN *C*ARE

> *Wedding gown fabrics are delicate and fragile. Therefore I recommend 3 points to ensure your gown is perfect before and after the wedding day. First, remove the dress from the hanger. Second, place the gown on a clean, white, cotton sheet lying it flat. Finally, fold the dress (with spotless white towels as a support) so the dress "rolls" and does not crease then lie flat on a shelf.*
>
> —Jonathan Scheer, Owner
> J. Scheer & Co. Wedding Gown Preservation, NY, NY
> www.jscheer.com

You and your husband are off on your honeymoon, so who is going to look after your beautiful wedding gown? Ask someone (your mother, an attendant) to get your dress to the cleaners immediately. The longer you wait, the more set any stains become and the harder they are to remove.

HELPFUL CLEANING HINTS

- Choose a reputable cleaner who is experienced in cleaning gowns. They are knowledgeable about removing stains like dirt, food, wine and champagne spills, and about handling fragile fabric.
- Remove shoulder pads and bra pads before cleaning. If your gown has fur trim, remove it before you take the dress to the cleaners.
- Ask if the cleaner uses acid-free tissue paper and an acid-free box for your gown.
- To do it yourself, place your gown in a 100% cotton garment bag and fold it neatly, don't hang it. Every year or so, unwrap the gown and refold it so the folds do not become permanent. Store in an acid-free box.
- Pack your headpiece and veil separately from the dress. The ornamentation on the headpiece contains adhesives that can cause browning.
- Place your gown in a low humidity, stable climate closet. Avoid basements and attics and never expose your gown to sunlight. The number one reason for "yellowing" is air exposure.
- If you get a stain on your dress, mask it with baby powder. Powder helps absorb the stain.
- Before you use hairspray, cover your shoulders with a clean white towel. Residue spray "settles" into the gown fabric.

CONCLUSION

Your wedding day is a new beginning to share life together and a close to your single days. It is a time of great emotion and feeling. It is not unusual to have thoughts of old friends and deceased loved ones. You may feel swept in a whirlwind one minute and feel like a bump on a log the next. Expect the unexpected and go with the flow. With proper planning and *My Bride Guide,* your wedding will be a joyful day that you will forever cherish.

Weddings account for an annual $70 billion business in the United States. Obviously, an industry this size provides plenty of options to choose from. As you do your homework, you will determine what is important to you and what is worthwhile compromising. In recent years weddings have gone from cake and champagne receptions to wedding weekend productions. Staying focused can become your biggest obstacle.

Take time to affirm your love and commitment to each other during this hectic time. The fiber of your relationship will grow into a rich tapestry as you communicate and respect each other with love. It's the little moments together that make the big moments great. Create special times to be together, watch a funny movie, share an ice cream sundae, or dance in the rain.

On your wedding day, take a few minutes together every half hour or so, to reflect on the beauty of the day. Literally, stop and smell the roses. Find a corner where you can observe your guests who share your joy. Step away for just a moment to catch your breath and celebrate the magic. Your wedding is a time to savor your moments together. May you be blessed with a wealth of love. May your days be bathed in light. May you live life from your heart. May you live in happiness and harmony, *till death do you part.*

ACKNOWLEDGMENTS

Writing a book is a lot like planning a wedding. It is a process, and the process requires patience and perseverance. When Barricade Books first approached me about writing a wedding planning book, my reaction was "a wedding planner, is this necessary?" But when I researched book sources and saw what existed I realized that such a book was not only necessary but also needed.

First, I wish to express my gratitude to the loyal support from Barricade Books, Inc. To Lyle Stuart and Carole Stuart whose vision and professionalism inspired me and kept me focused. To Jeff Nordstedt, a graphic wizard who gave an appealing style to plain text. To Heather Drummond, a dream editor who sent an encouraging card saying, "kick butt, you can do it," which had a profound effect on me when I felt like doing anything but write. Heather got married during the process of writing this book, which helped me keep the facts straight and the detail crisp. Also, to Paul Williams who has a true talent for listening and creating. To Marjorie Blum, whose promoting and marketing skill is the reason why you have this book.

Secondly, I wish to thank the many experts who allowed me to interview and quote them at the beginning of each chapter. Their solid advice allows any bride to feel confident. To Mokuba, a specialty store that stocks the most beautiful ribbons in the world. Their generosity resulted in an eye-popping book cover. To the brides, you deserve a bouquet of gratitude, to those that hired me and gave me access to your hearts and your stories.

Third, I am grateful to my dear friends and family who were always there for me – advising, mentoring, and sharing. To my brother, Ron whose "chat" with Dad resulted in

My Bride Guide, a title I love. To my brother Kevin who thrives on a good wedding story. To Mari Lyn Henry, Pauline Cornelius and Lynne Henderson who urged me to take risks and stand firmly for what I believe. To Edy Rose whose coaching sessions released my creative juices and stretched my imagination. To Stacey Schieffelin and Susie Galvez whose undying enthusiasm refueled me when I felt like giving up. They also convinced me to create cosmetics for the bride and showed me the steps to do it.

Finally, to my wonderful husband, Austin Graham, whose love and respect gave me the courage to start and finish this project. His sensitivity and playful spirit was the perfect antidote for my many overwhelming moments. To every bride and groom, may you have the blessing of magnificence in your marriage.

INDEX

INDEX